Advance Praise for *Choose Not to Fail*

"Must-read for anyone who manages others, is responsible for setting or executing on an organization's strategy, or just interested in personal and professional growth. Well written, fun to consume."

—Steve Cellini, former General Manager, Microsoft.
Founder Hyperbotic Labs, Inc.

"Peter Jerkewitz creates one compelling story after another. He brings simple analogies to life for practical use in being a more effective individual and working with others on your team. As I read his book, I kept coming up with questions—a good sign in itself. And the very next paragraph would then answer those very questions—a testament to the thoroughness and depth of each of his analogies. As an executive coach, I also strongly associated many of his examples with real-world leaders who are my clients. I kept thinking, I have to recommend that Paul read about Eating Crickets or Janice follow the advice in the Ball of Energy. This is definitely a book I plan to recommend to my leaders for practical use in their leadership journeys."

—Sabina Nawaz, Former Director, Microsoft.
Founder Nawaz Consulting

Published by
PonderWhy Inc.
Boston, MA

Publisher's Cataloging-in-Publication Data
Jerkewitz, Peter.

    Choose not to fail : 9 really smart behaviors you should bring to work every day / Peter Jerkewitz. – Boston, MA : PonderWhy Inc., 2012.

    p. ; cm.

    ISBN13: 978-0-9852797-0-7

    1. Teams in the work place. 2. Organizational communication. 3. Interactive management. 4. Corporate culture. I. Title.

    HD66.J47 2012
    658.402—dc22   2011962458

FIRST EDITION

Project coordination by Jenkins Group, Inc.
www.BookPublishing.com

Cover design by Chris Rhoads
Interior design by Brooke Camfield

Printed in the United States of America
16   15   14   13   12 • 5   4   3   2   1

Choose Not to Fail

9 Really Smart Behaviors You Should Bring to Work Every Day

Peter Jerkewitz

PonderWhy Inc.
Boston, MA

DEDICATION

This book is dedicated to Tammy, my sister and friend,
for her constant willingness to explore new ways of
thinking about so many ideas. This book, and your brother,
are both the better for knowing you.

Contents

ACKNOWLEDGMENTS

It is with great pride and deep respect that I get to thank so many smart, driven, and fun people for their influence, help, and insight in creating this book. What started as routine one-on-one mentoring meetings with people on my own teams has turned into something much greater. The stories in this book come from my creative process in communicating with the people I've worked with through the years. Each story was invented on the spur of the moment to help me communicate a focused idea with a specific person.

What my sister, Tammy Ouverson, helped me realize was that these simple stories actually had use far beyond my own meetings. When she started using them in her personal and professional life, the light bulb went on. Sis, I thank you so much for all your passion, insight, and drive to help bring this book into existence.

I learned many things on this book-writing journey. Early on, my good friend Ryan Sievers and I first explored in depth and breadth, on one written page, all the lessons each of these stories has to offer. In sharing them with Ryan, I came to grasp just how far these lessons can be utilized. Ryan, for your countless hours, passion, and true insight, I'll always be thankful.

A great number of wonderful people read draft after draft and provided fantastic insight. Your collective input helped me refine the message and present it in a way that is true to its original origin, the simple conversation between myself and a mentee. To that end, a special thanks to Elizabeth Alexander and Doug Fischer. Elizabeth, thank you for doing a full read of a very early draft. Your clear feedback helped me find the right tone and set-up to make the book work. Doug, thank you for your very detailed feedback on every chapter. You helped me polish the messages and bring order to the overall work. And to those who read, and in some cases re-read, chapter after chapter, I thank you as well. Your mark is too on this work.

I'd also like to thank the fine team at The Jenkins Group for all their help in the production of this book. Without your professionalism, passion, and clear dedication to creating great works, I'd never have made this happen. Your knowledge was pivotal in making this book a great deal more than just a collection of stories.

And Gwen. How do I thank Gwen Moran? While I provided the ideas and concepts for this effort, Gwen contributed as the ghostwriter. Gwen, you so adeptly brought my vision and voice to life in the written word. You masterfully steered us through numerous drafts until it was just right. You gave fantastic input on focusing messages and keeping the flow moving well. This book has your handprint on it, and I'm so fortunate for that. Thank you in so, so many ways.

And last, but really first in my mind, thank you to the teams and people with whom I've had the great opportunity to work. It's in our daily interactions, in our one-on-one meetings, and in my work with each of you that I saw these stories and came to find myself as a communicator who uses stories to share complex ideas. I'm happy to know these stories have lasting impact, and again, I thank my past colleagues for the opportunity to find myself in such a creative way.

Chapter 1

A Stronger Business through Simple, Meaningful Stories

Business leaders worldwide are battle-scarred today, coping with one of the worst economic downturns in history as a volatile global economy continuously presents threats on many fronts. Technology is changing virtually everything about the way we do business. Uncertainty is the new "normal" and we are learning to navigate a paradoxical business environment that is fraught with peril and rich with opportunity. The key to success is making the right choices. But how?

Caught in the middle of such a volatile time, it can be difficult to differentiate threats from opportunities. Where does it make sense to take on more risk as opposed to playing it safe? Will being prudent cause you to miss out on a potentially big win? Will you be a hero for safely navigating stormy waters? The answers depend on the circumstances, of course. But questions such as these leave business owners desperately searching for ways to control the chaos.

Although most of us can't control many of the external factors that affect our businesses, we should be focusing on what we can control,

1

stripping away the drama and bringing a new level of clarity grounded in reality and good business practices rather than in panic and illusion. By sharpening our focus on things we *can* influence, the next best move becomes clearer.

Storytelling has long been a tool that leaders have used to simplify complexities and pass on lessons in a non-threatening and engaging way. It's through nine such stories that this book delivers insights into common business mistakes that drain resources and productivity. These parables, or adages, distill perennial business problems to their basics and offer strategies and tactics to diffuse and eliminate them. In so doing, the book becomes your personal mentor—a source of counsel and insight that can prepare you to make better choices and find opportunities within even the most chaotic circumstances.

This ability to effectively and selectively manage challenges and motivate people will, over time, make or break a company's performance in the marketplace. Whether in the form of company departments or groups of talented individuals brought together for specific projects or tasks, working with teams requires navigating interpersonal dynamics and priorities on a daily basis. People have a wide range of skills and abilities, individual personal and professional goals, and unique personality types. This very distinct combination effectively creates a set of filters through which each of us processes information. In turn, it creates a complex communications challenge in any team. At best, navigating this challenge can be tricky. At worst, it can derail your momentum entirely.

Collectively, the nine stories and the discussion surrounding them will help you and your team accomplish a key goal: you'll be able to make more conscious, eyes-wide-open choices in several critical areas. You'll have a greater awareness of the factors motivating your people and their actions and a better understanding of how we interact with those around us—and of what things we should always be aware. With more conscious choices and clear communication, we can make better data-driven decisions for the good of all. By enabling better communication of the choices and intentions with the people around us, we'll inspire our teams to perform better while cultivating happier, more engaged employees. In short, in these critical key areas, we can consciously and effectively *choose not to fail.*

Meet the Mentor

As you read this book, you'll get to know Blake Richards. Blake is an organizational consultant who is frequently called upon to manage change and to help individuals operate more effectively in a team environment—again, helping people keep their eyes wide open as they face choices and challenges. Before going off on his own, Blake was a manager in a large company with a track record of organizing and running effective teams. Eventually, he became the go-to person for troubleshooting problems that teams were experiencing anywhere in the company. He decided to take his team management skills and apply them to a variety of companies through his consulting practice. Beyond the workplace, Blake is simply the kind of person to whom people usually feel comfortable turning for advice.

You'll also be introduced to Kate Wallace. She's a high-performing junior manager, well on her way to a very fulfilling and influential career within her industry. She's been in her industry for a little more than 10 years, managing teams for a little more than six. Within the last year, she received her latest promotion and stepped into the role of supervising managers—a new responsibility for her. She turned to an old college professor with whom she'd been keeping in touch for some guidance on how best to take on this new role while continuing to look to the future regarding her own career. That professor, of course, introduced Kate to Blake.

Through a series of conversations between Blake and his latest mentee, you will be introduced to several analogies that can help you work effectively with and within teams. While you'll find each analogy fits different situations, they do have a common thread running through them: consciousness. When you're not fully aware of the interactions going on around you, you can't make the best decisions for yourself, your teammates, or those you are supervising. However, when you're tuned in to the potential for these energy- and engagement-draining pitfalls, you can create positive change in both your business and your personal life.

The next time you find yourself in a team at work or doing an activity with those around you at home, keep an eye out for one or more of these challenging situations to rear its head. You'll be surprised how often it happens, as well as how easily most can be diffused and dismissed. What many teams don't realize is that recognizing these situations and managing them will make any team a lot more effective in trying situations.

For example, when team plans are not spelled out clearly and objectives are not clearly defined, wasted energy and confusion almost always ensue. Communicating in ways that are in tandem with the needs and proclivities of team members can do wonders in helping your team create the desired results.

A second example: people often fall into patterns of assumptions when it comes to interacting with those on their team and determining how they will collectively accomplish their goals. It's natural that team members with varying skills and personalities differ in their styles of work and communication. One might be a visionary who can't be bothered with details—the antithesis of a quiet and reserved team member who needs to know exactly how a plan will be executed. Another may be an extrovert who can talk a mile a minute, much to the dismay of an introverted teammate, who needs time and quiet to process ideas.

This is where assumptions are problematic. If we assume that everyone abides by the same conventional wisdom on how to behave and how projects will get done, productivity will suffer. Tell the extrovert to "be quiet" and you've effectively shut down her method of thinking through ideas. Tell the big-idea person to write a report that spells out how to execute his concepts and he'll likely be mired in a sea of self-doubt and confusion. By understanding the dynamics of how individuals function in team settings, you can spot the extrovert who just needs a few minutes to talk through an idea or the detail-oriented team member who gets overwhelmed when big ideas aren't supported by specific operational elements.

It's no surprise that each of these people will likely view a given situation differently. They can all see the elephant, but each from his or her unique point of view. Some see the hind legs, others the trunk, and still others the rough skin covering the great animal. Add to the example the urgency for the team to actually get work done. If team members have wavering confidence but don't want to admit they need help, the situation is ripe for miscommunication, errant assumptions, and frustrated, sometimes even angry, participants.

Again, this is where analogies are helpful. Creating shortcuts to understanding what's going on in front of us allows many individual and team challenges to be simplified. Even more powerfully, using the brief names of these analogies in conversation allows complex concepts to be instantly communicated and quickly understood. By increasing awareness in this way about common team challenges, teams become more knowledgeable about potential pitfalls and more effective overall in working together. Best of all, they are more likely to realize that, collectively, they're all seeing an elephant, and that one person's point of view is as needed and as valuable as the next.

Chapter 2

EVERYONE'S HOMETOWN
MAKES THE BEST PIZZA

Blake walked into the coffee shop to find Kate already sitting at their usual table. To his surprise, she was wearing a sweatshirt emblazoned with the Penn State logo, a relic from her undergraduate days.

"A bit casual for the office, no?" Blake joked.

"Very funny," she smiled. "I'm working from home today to catch up on some paperwork, but I'm glad we could meet for coffee."

"Well, being reminded that you went to Penn State could make me change my mind. Michigan has always been the better team."

"Hey, watch it. I'm very protective of my alma mater and Nittany Lions football. This could lead to an argument," she said, half smiling.

"You know, sometimes that happens, and when it does it impacts your teams work output too. And more often than you might think, because everyone's hometown makes the best pizza," said Blake.

"That sounds like one of your analogies."

"Well, as a matter of fact, it is. Interested in hearing more about Pizza Statements?" Blake offered.

"You bet. I'm sure we'll even figure out how they fit into this crazy world of mine."

Jane's Pet Project

Inspired to make a positive difference in her office's environmental impact, Jane Anderson took it upon herself to research an in-house recycling program. She spent hours of her own time researching best practices and developing a program. Within a few weeks, after getting approval from her supervisor, she had set up recycling systems for paper, glass, and plastic. She felt good about helping her company reduce waste and be more green.

A few weeks after the program launched, Jane was in a meeting with Dan Frost, the vice president of marketing. The marketing team was looking for new publicity for the company. Jane reminded them of the recycling program's success and suggested that a news release about the program would help bolster the company's green image. The team liked the idea.

Dan quietly whispered to Jane, "You know, if you really want to see a good recycling program, you should talk to my brother. His company is the best—they even won an award for their program. I'll get you his phone number. Tell him I told you to call and get a few pointers."

Jane couldn't believe the criticism she was hearing, but she didn't want to make a scene in front of the other team members. Red-faced, she stammered, "S-sure. Thanks." She remained silent for the rest of the meeting and rushed out the door as soon as it was over.

Her thoughts tumbled over each other as she walked quickly back to her desk. *How could he insinuate that I need to look to other programs for guidance? Does he have any idea how much work I've put into this program? Work that isn't part of my job responsibilities? What does he mean, "Get a few pointers"? Is he saying my program isn't good?*

"I doubt he even knows one detail of how this program works," she fumed.

Meanwhile, Dan had a much different take. He was surprised Jane hadn't contributed more in the second half of the meeting, but he wrote it off to having a bad day. Then he reminded himself to give his brother a head's up about Jane's call and encourage him to share as much information as he could with her. Dan felt certain his brother would be able to give her some good ideas that would make her recycling coordinator job easier. He thought Jane had done a great job starting and growing the program, and she might be able to help his brother as well. He felt as though this would be a valuable introduction for each of them.

Blake, who had witnessed the meeting, Jane's response, and Dan's obliviousness, knew he had his work cut out for him. Both individuals clearly had a lot to learn about pizza.

What Really Happened?
A Pizza Statement Got in the Way

If you asked Dan and Jane about their perspectives of the conversation, you would get two completely different takes. Jane felt slighted and couldn't get Dan's uninformed comments out of her head.

Dan was pleased he'd made a connection, but he was also surprised when Jane ended up being so quiet and reserved during the meeting. He even began to question whether she was adding value to his program. Maybe she was too distracted with this recycling program?

However, what actually happened was that he'd competed with her on an off-topic item and his perceived insult had made her angry, which diminished her ability to focus and her willingness to participate.

The classic miscommunication that occurred in this case lies in the assumption that one program has to be better than another, or even worse, is has to be the "best."

Most of us naturally associate ourselves with worthwhile challenges. We want to be successful in the areas where we devote our time. That's why employee studies repeatedly show that praise and recognition are powerful tools when it comes to engagement and retention. However, that engagement can be undermined by inadvertent comments that indicate one person—or his or her associations—is better than another. Such comments may not be significant to the person who utters them, but saying something is the "best" or "better than" sets up a competition that can undermine the actual purpose for a meeting, project, or initiative.

This happens often, even when we don't realize it. The offending attitudes can range from playful banter between sports fans about which team is better to outright elitist or narrow-minded attitudes about which homes, backgrounds, and possessions are best.

Of course, you've probably known people who good-naturedly knock their hometown or the state in which they grew up. They may make fun of their birthplace, its sports teams, and its stereotypes. But if you ever try to make a similar joke, it often doesn't go over well. Why is that? It's not as if the place is sacred—you may have heard your friend or co-worker knock New Jersey, Iowa, or Texas dozens of times before. But when you try to do it, you're met with defensiveness, even if your comment is good-natured, and typically you're treated to an accounting of what is actually great about the city or state or ball team. And, of course, the food, because everyone's hometown does, in fact, make the best pizza.

We see the same dynamic in business. When one person or team declares someone or something "the best," that creates a win/loss situation in which everyone else is *not* the best. It creates the same type of defensiveness as criticizing a member of someone's family. Because people usually feel such deep affinity for their work and internalize how they do those jobs as measures of their worth, the thought that it may be less than excellent is counterproductive. The less-than-best employees may lose their enthusiasm if they feel as though they've been slighted and unappreciated. They may even expend negative energy arguing the point that, in fact, they are better than people realize. Obviously, while Pizza Statements may seem benign, they are often problematic in very serious ways.

There's great pressure on us to be the "best." It's part of our culture. How many times have you heard, "Be anything you want to be—just give it your best," which we all too often internalize as "Be the best"? In business, in sports, and in life, we're repeatedly told there's no place for second best; it's coming in first that matters. We all want to be involved with the greatest, but the only way to be the best is for someone else to be less than best.

By not realizing that Jane was heavily invested in her program and framing his suggestion that she reach out for more information in a way that indicated he was trying to help her and make her job easier, Dan accidentally insulted her. The result was wasted energy and a decline in productivity. The net effect is that Dan picked a fight, even though he may not have realized it and certainly didn't intend to do so. The inadvertent comparison of the two programs had no place at all in that meeting.

In a corporate setting, you're often going to find Pizza Statements. When you do, the best way to diffuse them is to bring the team to a higher level of common ground. For example, instead of being two separate teams, find the goal toward which all the teams are working. Or, emphasize that two teams can, and often do, "make great pizza."

In hindsight, Dan would have been more effective had he avoided using comparisons altogether. Instead of creating a situation in which his brother's recycling program was "better," he could simply have said that his brother had launched an excellent recycling program as well and perhaps they could share ideas. By avoiding superlatives, he could have made a valuable connection without making Jane feel insulted or threatened. Such a connection isn't a slight—it creates common ground and may have even been met with enthusiasm.

Conversely, had Jane been trained to spot a Pizza Statement, she could have avoided a great deal of negative energy and wasted time. Instead of feeling as if Dan was denigrating her work, she could have recognized that he was using the Pizza Statement in an effort to generate her enthusiasm about how his brother could help her with a project that was clearly important to her. Dan had no intention of insulting her and, in fact, had left the meeting feeling pretty good about himself and how his brother and Jane would be able to help each other, though he was conscious of Jane's lack of input.

Had she been able to look beyond the superficial meaning of the words to his true intent, she would have seen that what he meant to do was almost the polar opposite of what she perceived.

How to Handle Pizza Statements

When someone says their hometown has the best cheese or best pizza or best bagels or best coffee, your immediate reaction may be, "You're wrong! *My* town has the best!" accompanied, of course, by an air of indignation. When someone claims a "best" vacation spot or car or color or sports team, that is a clear statement that he or she feels that all others are inferior to that choice. Such things may be said in jest, but they can be insulting to others who don't share that view.

Nonetheless, it's important not to disagree with Pizza Statements. Just as it's practically impossible to tell someone from Chicago that New York has better pizza than the Windy City, you're going to have a tough time convincing the "pizza" employee that his or her statement isn't true. When an employee or team lays claim to being the best, positively reinforce him or her in a way that reaches for the higher ground.

It's often more effective to acknowledge the statement, which is rarely made with the negativity with which it is perceived. For example, in Jane's case, had she understood that Dan's statement was just a Pizza Statement instead of a denigration of her efforts, she could have more easily dismissed it and possibly even benefited from getting new ideas from Dan on what value he saw in his brother's approach. Such statements are frequently careless or made without a conscious intent, but that doesn't mean they need to be received in the same way.

In any workplace, it's important to find ways to make accomplishments and contributions known without alienating others. This kind of self-promotion doesn't come easily for everyone, but it's essential to safeguard your reputation as a valuable contributor to your company and your team.

However, there's a difference between confidently sharing successes and achievements and the bravado that comes with ego-pumping at the expense of valuing others' contributions. The latter is where Pizza Statements can be problematic. They may seem simple and harmless at first, but the more they take root, the more they foster a culture of negative competition, resentment, and hostility that needs to be overcome.

Pizza Statements can be extremely destructive, so learn how to recognize them and better understand the intent behind them. Instead of expending energy on conflicts that don't matter and that may not even be "real," remember that many Pizza Statements are often borne out of pre-meeting banter rather than with the intention of creating conflict. By looking for ways to use Pizza Statements to connect and define priorities and intentions, they can actually be a helpful tool in team building.

Kate's Home Team

Kate nodded as she considered this new perspective.

"I've seen that happen often. When someone says something is 'the best,' it's almost a challenge that they know more than you do or they don't value your opinion of what's best. Or, like our discussion about teams, we have a personal connection and when our team isn't 'the best,' we take it to heart," Kate said.

"That's right."

"So how can you best defuse a Pizza Statement?"

"Remember to recognize the contribution each side has made, reduce any negative fallout from the statement, and move on. After all, how often are these statements simply the verbal equivalent of chest-pounding or humorous fidgeting, adding no real value to the conversation?" Blake asked.

"The bottom line is, you don't want yourself or your teammates to compete or focus on things that don't move the team and the business forward," he explained. "If you're spending energy on meaningless competition, you're diverting it from where it should go: toward creating better results."

"But how do you handle situations where someone makes a Pizza Statement that's entirely off-base?" Kate asked.

"Well, it's true that some people have an inaccurate perspective of their contributions to the company's success. However, rather than stomping on the employee for this misperception, use it as a valuable teaching opportunity. Clearly, some kind of communication isn't working if the employee has such a misperception of his or her role in the company. It may be time for a performance review where specific goals and strategies for improvement are discussed. Perhaps additional training is in order. Look for ways to channel the enthusiasm employees have about being the best into ways that allow them to actually improve their skills."

"But the bottom line is to recognize and neutralize the statement and then move on," Kate concluded.

"That's it."

"Except for one thing."

"What's that?"

"Penn State really is better than Michigan," she grinned.

Chapter 3

THE BALL OF ENERGY

Blake walked slowly to a table in the front of the coffee shop, carefully carrying two cups of coffee. As he looked up, he saw Kate enter the shop and walk to their regular table, nearly bumping into another customer. She absentmindedly threw off her coat and sat down.

Blake handed her the coffee and she took a long sip.

"Thanks. I needed that."

"Something on your mind?" he asked.

"Well, you know we're going through this reorganization. Everyone's been under a lot of pressure. But today, our area vice president came in and informed some of the managers that their offices would be moved. Steve, who's a team leader on one of our big projects, got really angry and walked out of the meeting."

"That's interesting. Does he usually get upset over changes like this?"

"No, he's usually pretty level-headed. I think the stress is getting to him. All I know is he'd better toughen up or he's never going to get through this."

"That's true. You know Kate, I find when people do things that seem way out of character, it's often driven by something that's not obvious to the casual observer."

"What do you mean?"

"Well, you said Steve is usually pretty calm and even-tempered. I mean, given how you've spoken of him in our previous conversations, his actions today seem out of character with his personality. That tells me there might be something else going on. This news was likely meaningful to him in ways that aren't necessarily obvious," said Blake. "It's important that, as a leader, if you want to help, you need to consider more what caused him to react this way rather than the reaction itself."

"I suppose you're right," Kate mused. "What do you think it could be?"

"Well, I'm not sure, but it's fairly clear that he got hit with a Ball of Energy," Blake replied.

"What's that? One of those new caffeine drinks?"

Blake laughed. "No, it sounds like Steve was hit with a change he didn't expect—the Ball of Energy—and for him, it's probably not simply the change of his office moving. His response to having his office moved may be a symptom of something else . . . Something bigger that's having an impact on him."

Kate smiled. "Clearly, you've seen this before."

"You bet," Blake said, returning her grin.

"How about telling me more about how this Ball of Energy works?"

"Gladly," Blake replied. "Brace yourself: you're about to hear the tale of Jack Sullivan and the Ball of Energy he had to manage." He took a sip of his coffee and began.

Jack Sullivan and the Ball of Energy

For weeks, Jack had been managing a reorganization of the sales and marketing departments of CompuCorp, the multinational computer hardware manufacturer where he is vice president of marketing. Lately, he'd been losing sleep over the prospect of informing Sarah, one of his employees, of her imminent layoff.

Anyone who ever met Sarah knew immediately that she loved her job. She loved being the leader of the department. She was always excited and engaged whenever she talked about her job and her team. However, her performance hadn't been as stellar as many had expected. While she had some strong skills, she simply wasn't growing with the position, and the position was growing.

Jack recognized her talent, and had spent quite a bit of focused time coaching and mentoring her. Still he knew she would need to be let go as part of the reorganization, because of her slower growth. He felt worse when he thought of the new house she and her husband had recently purchased. While his pragmatism usually helped him make tough decisions, this one weighed on him more than usual.

One sleepless night, he found an answer: he thought of a way to add a position to the department that would capitalize on Sarah's strengths and possibly revive her future with CompuCorp. He went to his desk at 2:00 a.m. and wrote out a job description after revising the organizational chart. Even though the process took the rest of the night, he felt great—revitalized and relieved—the next day.

That is, until he met with Sarah to explain the situation to her. He ran into her in the hallway and couldn't wait to share his vision with her, sure she'd be crazy successful in this new role. She was glad to see him, too.

"Hi, Jack! Listen, I wanted to talk to you. My review is coming up and I've been prepping for it." She broke into a wide grin. "I'm going to make a strong case for a fat raise, my friend."

Jack paused. She didn't know how close she'd come to losing her job, and clearly still hadn't heard the feedback given over the past few months on some areas of her performance. Even though, he believed in being honest and direct, so he decided he'd better manage her expectations a little. On the spur of the moment, he decided to tell her immediately about the changes coming her way.

"Sarah, listen. I've got a few things to discuss with you about the reorg," he began.

"Okay. Is there anything I should know in advance of our meeting?" she asked, cautious after hearing his tone.

Jack took a deep breath, and pulled her aside. "Look, I know how hard you've worked. But we feel like this department should be going in a different direction. We're going to take advantage of this reorganization to expand the director role and bring in a more senior person than we've had in the past. So, I'm sorry, but we're going to move you out of your position. But I've created a new position for you under the new director, who will be brought in from the outside."

Jack's voice now rang with enthusiasm. Finally, he'd gotten the news off his chest, and in any event it was good news. After all, it was such a good fit for Sarah!

She looked stunned. "A new position?"

"It's actually exciting news, Sarah. I think you'll see that, in the long run, it's for the best," he faltered, a bit surprised at her reaction.

"For the best?" Sarah's face grew red with anger. "Really? You think that taking me out of a job that I've had for two years—and, might I add, have done very well at—and demoting me is for the best? I don't see how you could think that, Jack!"

"Sarah, come on. Let's look at this objectively," Jack said.

"Objectively? Are you kidding? You've sandbagged me in the middle of the hallway and you think I'm not being objective? I think I've had enough of this conversation." She quickly turned and walked away.

Jack muttered under his breath, "Well, that went pretty well, didn't it?"

Minutes later, a bit dazed, he walked past Blake's office. Then he paused and wandered in.

Blake looked up and immediately realized something was wrong.

"What's up, Jack? You don't look so good."

Jack slumped in a chair and explained what had happened.

"I don't get it," he implored when he finished the doleful tale. "It's actually good news. I mean, I didn't want to do this. It's for the good of the department. She should see that. And I'm not actually laying her off, which was about to happen." He ran his hands through his hair.

"I appreciate that the company needs to do this," Jack continued, "but I have to tell you, Blake, I just despise the feeling of being a hatchet man. I feel better now that I don't have to keep this big secret to myself, but it's still hard."

Managing the Ball of Energy

Alas, it's a familiar dynamic. Jack had been struggling with some of the decisions that he needed to make during the reorganization, which was the largest he'd ever handled. After working for years with many of the people who were going to be affected, he felt personally responsible for their well-being. During the reorganization, some people would lose their jobs or be reassigned—necessary changes to cut costs and improve efficiency. Jack, of course, felt extreme stress over the prospect of unsettling his colleagues' lives so dramatically, and the pressure began affecting his home life. It was all he could think or talk about.

Change is never easy, especially when it's going to mean difficult news for some of the people you really care for, but it comes with the territory. And many times, in the end, it's not as bad as you think it's going to be.

Jack was responsible for delivering life-changing news. It's natural in such cases that a great deal of expectant energy develops. He was under a great deal of stress, trying to figure out how to pass on the news. With the information finally delivered, he initially felt a great sense of relief. For him, this big step in his journey was largely over.

However, the person receiving the news has now been launched on her own sudden and unexpected journey. She has to figure out what has happened and what it all means.

That's what happened when Jack passed the news of the reorganization along to Sarah. While before he'd been agonizing over the prospect of telling her she would lose her job, he was suddenly internally enthusiastic and happy because not only was he finally getting the news out, he'd come up with an ingenious solution to move her into a new role.

By contrast, in an instant, he'd given Sarah all the energy of the very same news that had caused him so much anxiety for so long, and this news had changed everything in her world.

It's hard to think of a better example of the Ball of Energy than this.

Round Two of How Jack Managed His Ball of Energy

"Well, what should I do about it?" Jack asked, now that he understood that a new and personal journey had just begun for his employee.

"You need to go follow up to make sure she's calming down and not reactively on the phone to the first headhunter who will take her call," Blake said.

Immediately, Jack went to find Sarah.

When he knocked on the door of her office, he was relieved to hear her say, "Come in."

"Hey, Sarah. I just wanted to follow up on our talk earlier today. I regret that it was so heated," he said.

"I don't think there's anything left to say, Jack. I work hard for this company and this is the thanks I get? You think that I'm going to stay here and just take this? I don't think so." Sarah's face reddened and her voice rose.

Jack tried to calm her down. "Sarah, I know you're upset. Just think it over before you make any rash decisions."

"You know, Jack, I thought we were friends," said Sarah. "You really disappoint me."

"I know I surprised you today, and I wish I had delivered the news a bit better." Jack's

voice was conciliatory and genuine. "But please do sleep on this and think through what your new role would be before you make any decisions. I really do think it'd be a fantastic fit for you." With that, he let himself out of her office and returned to Blake to relay part two of the story.

Blake wasn't surprised.

"That's a pretty common reaction from someone who has just received a big Ball of Energy. It's important not to take what she's say ing personally, Jack. She probably doesn't mean it. She's just processing this massive amount of information. All the energy of those sleepless nights and all the tension you felt for days—for weeks, actually—has now been handed off to her, in a blink" Blake explained.

"It's always important to give the catcher of the Ball of Energy time to process it," he continued. "All the uncertainty and anxiety caused by change is now in Sarah's hands. She's probably worried about the lost money, position, and responsibilities. Her ego is also likely bruised. And while you've had time to resolve your struggle, Sarah's has just begun. She's trying to sort out a situation that feels like rejection. She may have been counting on a promotion and raise, and now she needs to reconcile that neither is happening, and that the path she had laid out in her head is taking a detour."

Jack nodded, and Blake concluded, "These are all challenging realizations, and Sarah will need time to figure out a way to cope with them, just as it took you time to get over the anxiety you felt at the news."

How to Successfully Manage a Ball of Energy

There are a number of things Jack could have done to better manage this situation. First, he shouldn't have sprung the news on Sarah in such a casual way. It would have been less awkward if he had managed himself better and waited until their formal meeting.

He might also have given her some indication that they would be discussing the reorganization so that she wasn't blindsided by the restructuring news. He might have hinted that changes were coming so that Sarah was less surprised. Sometimes, by "dripping" news, team members can get clues that things may change, giving them a chance to think about what such changes might mean. Often, they will come up with a worst-case scenario on their own and may even begin coming up with a plan to deal with it. At the least, hints give them an initial exposure to such ideas on their own, making them less shocking when received from someone else.

Several techniques can be used to share big, unexpected news. However, not all techniques work in every situation. Jack would have been more effective had he spent some time thinking about the situation from Sarah's point of view. For her, what would be the best way to deliver this news? Should it be delivered verbally or also in writing? How exactly should he explain it? And when? Early in the day, at a formal meeting, with the remainder of the day left to process it, or at an informal meeting over coffee?

The circumstances surrounding the message is as important as the message itself. The main question is, how could Jack have increased

Sarah's comfort level and made the news easier to receive? He can't not deliver it, but how could he have helped Sarah best receive this Ball of Energy?

It turned out, Sarah needed some time away from the situation in order to process it. Fortunately, the weekend was at hand, and she spent a lot of time thinking about her situation. On Monday morning, she stopped by the temporary office that had been Blake's home base during the reorganization and they had a very pleasant conversation.

Later that day, she welcomed Jack when he stopped by her office and explained more details about the new position. Her outlook had changed considerably, and she was elated to realize she'd be heading up the art department, which was her favorite part of the job anyway. Basically, she realized, she was going to be doing all the things she liked and getting rid of all the things she didn't like, including twelve-hour days. She was even able to negotiate a title change and a small raise. Once she had the full picture, plus the time to process it, she could see this was a really good opportunity.

Sarah's experience with the Ball of Energy has happened to each of us at one time or another. Perhaps not in losing a job, but we've all been blindsided by news or a change that was totally unexpected and/or delivered in a brusque, careless fashion. We are frequently the recipients of big news, only some of which is good. It's hard when we get hit with a Ball of Energy, but with understanding, we can better and more readily process such events. Ask yourself: how can you best prepare for the unexpected Balls of Energy that will inevitably come your way?

For starters, know your own processing method for dealing with this kind of information. When you get hit, move quickly to that strategy. Maybe you'll want to ask for time to think and go for a walk. Maybe you'll want to get input from your closest friends and family members. Perhaps you'll want to sit down and write about it.

Whatever your preference, do engage in whatever allows you to deal with the sudden energy while you contemplate how you'll respond in the long run. You don't want to allow the Ball of Energy to consume you and cause you to react in ways that you'll regret down the road.

On the flip side, those who are about to deliver a Ball of Energy feel anxiety, excitement, and pent-up energy as they anticipate the reactions of others. Once the news is delivered, they usually feel better. The burden of expectation is relieved. Remember to think about how the specific individual hearing it will best receive the news. Think about how he or she will likely respond, and how to avoid reacting to their initial words and actions. Give them room to absorb what's going on in that minute. Remember, the receiver is at square one when it comes to dealing with the energy, so help this person along!

Kate's Ball of Energy

"That's some story," Kate said. "It all worked out in the end, though?"

"It did. But it would have gone smoother if Jack had realized that he was about to toss a Ball of Energy and had prepared for it a bit better. This was news that would be disruptive to Sarah. And it also would have gone better had she understood the concept of the Ball of Energy and had processed the situation more effectively."

"So, you're thinking that Steve's reaction wasn't about the office, but maybe something else, and that he needs time to process it," Kate mused.

"That definitely sounds like the case," said Blake. "His reaction of storming out of the room seems a bit too extreme for just an office move. But maybe it is the office. He clearly needed time to process something not necessarily obvious, and didn't want to explode there in the room."

Kate stared out the window and began to see how she could use the concept of the Ball of Energy to better manage her own team. With the company's upcoming reorganization, she knew there would be plenty of big news items for her team. Clearly, she needed to find ways to help them prepare for and manage those Balls of Energy.

She suddenly looked back to Blake.

"Is the Ball of Energy always bad news?"

"Oh no, not at all," Blake smiled. "People who have received a promotion, a new job offer, or even news of a baby on the way have been passed a Ball of Energy. Their heads may be reeling with the news and the way it will change their work and home lives. This may cause a dip in productivity or a feeling of being overwhelmed for a period after the news is delivered," he explained.

"It's really about the degree or amount of change," he added, "and not as much about the good news/bad news aspect, though it often takes us longer to internalize and process big balls of energy that turn out to be bad news. Remember, in Jack's case, he may have felt he was passing along a ball of positive energy—after all, he'd found a way to move Sarah within the company instead of letting her go entirely."

"But she certainly didn't take it that way," Kate replied.

"No, and can you see why?"

"Absolutely. And I guess there are times when a Ball of Energy could be good news and bad news. Say a supervisor you like takes a new job elsewhere and you're going to be promoted to that position. You're happy at the opportunity, but maybe scared about the challenge and sad that someone you like is leaving," she said.

"Now you're getting it," Blake said. "You always need to be aware of the impact the ball is having on the catcher and others around you. In Sarah's case, she was being taken out of her job and, essentially, moved to a job with less responsibility. That's a very discouraging situation to someone who is hardworking and ambitious. By her measure, she'd been successful, and now she felt as though she wasn't being properly recognized for her efforts. Clearly, the news she received didn't fit the expectation she had. She was probably angry and felt like she wanted to retaliate or prove that she was right and should be kept in the position she'd had. Now she was in the position of trying to figure out what to do with this big Ball of Energy."

"But you can't always predict how people will respond," Kate pointed out.

"True," Blake replied. "People have different reasons why a given Ball of Energy affects them one way or the other. If Sarah had been looking for a less stressful job that would allow her to focus more on the art she loved, this Ball of Energy would have been pure bliss to her."

Both Kate and Blake reflected on this for a moment, and then Blake spoke again.

"One other thought: an important key to managing a Ball of Energy is to effectively anticipate the size it will be when it's received. Exactly how big is the challenge, opportunity, or change that's being transferred? Look through the eyes of the recipient," he advised. "Larger Balls of Energy require more preparation and effort to resolve than small Balls of Energy. For example, if a team knows that reorganization happens at the end of every product cycle, the Ball of Energy is likely smaller. They know the reorganization is coming and can anticipate it."

Kate nodded.

"However, if an individual is moved from a team mid-project with no warning, either to take on a new project or because he or she isn't performing as expected, that's a much bigger disruption and requires more energy to manage."

Blake smiled. "Finally, the size of the Ball of Energy is also related to what the receiver values. In Sarah's case, her job was an important part of how she identified herself. Losing that job meant more than just a transfer of responsibilities. It was a criticism of her performance and the delay of a promotion she felt she deserved. She saw it as a setback in her career to be reassigned to something unknown. Combined, those factors represented a very large Ball of Energy for her. To be blindsided on top of such a loss made Sarah's angry reaction more predictable."

Kate's Conundrum

Kate looked thoughtful. "You've hit the nail on the head. This must be what's going on with Steve. For him, this is something different than maybe it is for the rest of us."

"It sounds like it," Blake agreed. "The Ball of Energy can come in a variety of different forms. It can even come from a third party. Perhaps it's a confidence that is shared with you about a co-worker or friend that indirectly affects or concerns you. Rumors can create powerful Balls of Energy. Learning about an employer's plans to relocate to a new state before the information is public knowledge could easily cause stress and anxiety. Remember, sometimes people relay Balls of Energy without meaning to do so," Blake finished.

"Right. I can see how even some inquiries about a prospective change—like your boss asking questions about a new way of doing things—could lead people to speculate and worry about their jobs. Or if someone tells you something in confidence that will affect you, but you can't really say anything about it because you're bound by the confidentiality. What happens in those cases, when you're the one hit with the Ball of Energy?"

"You need to compose yourself quickly. Your professionalism and options for what you might want to do can be damaged if you react too emotionally before considering all aspects. The last thing you want to do is damage relationships. Find a way to think through the situation and its real and potential outcomes before you take a stand," Blake answered.

"That's where Steve had an issue."

"Exactly. Sounds like he let the Ball of Energy overwhelm him. My guess, or shall I say my hope, is that he'll be back in short order, far more composed."

"Do you really think that will happen?"

"It's hard to say for certain. The Ball of Energy can be tricky to manage if you don't take time to see it in play. But once you do, it can really help. When you get hit by one, you can more quickly compose yourself and react responsibly to the real situation. Oftentimes you'll realize the 'sender' can't really avoid passing along the Ball of Energy or didn't mean it the way the receiver perceived it. As a manager, you need to think thoroughly about how to help others receive information that will be disruptive. You can think about timing, exact messaging, and how you empower them to step into the journey you know they are about to begin. Simply respecting and being sensitive to the fact that the news you'll share will thrust them into a sudden journey they likely weren't expecting will take you far and make you a stronger leader. It's not easy," Blake admitted. "Each case is different. But the skills necessary to deliver a Ball of Energy are always the same."

Kate considered this for a moment. "This discussion has cleared up some of my recent confusion about my colleagues. I admit, I'm somewhat anxious to put this one into play back at the office with my team. And, of course, to reach out to Steve and gently see if there's anything I can do to help him as he processes his Ball of Energy."

Blake grinned as they stood to leave. "Great—and don't forget those at home too. We have plenty of Balls of Energy being tossed back and forth there, too."

Chapter 4

MANAGING YOUR TOKENS

Blake was on a train to a client meeting in Boston when his mobile phone rang. He looked at the screen and saw it was Kate.

"To what do I owe this pleasant surprise?" he answered.

"Blake, do you have a minute?"

Kate sounded distressed.

"I have an issue I need to discuss."

"Of course, Kate. What's going on?"

"I dropped the ball on an assignment. I can't believe it. I was in a meeting two weeks ago and one of the division vice presidents asked me to run a few reports for him. Well, to be honest, I was in back-to-back meetings that day and I didn't get a chance to review my notes until yesterday. I realized that he needed the reports for a big meeting today, so my assistant, Carrie, and I stayed until midnight last night running them."

"That doesn't sound like dropping the ball to me."

"It gets worse. The numbers in the report are from the wrong quarter, and there are several glaring typos I didn't catch because I was so tired.

When I noticed them this morning, after we'd sent them to my boss's boss, I hit the roof. The minute Carrie got to work, I called her into my office. I was angry and spoke very sharply to her, telling her she needed to be more careful in the future. She didn't say anything, but I could tell she was really upset."

"Okay. Go on."

"Well, when I looked back over the instructions I gave Carrie, it turns out that it was all my fault. I told her to run the wrong numbers. Plus, I have to admit that she's usually so meticulous that I didn't really proofread the reports that carefully. Now the management team will question our competence and Carrie is angry. Boy, I really messed up."

"Well, first of all, you need to stop beating yourself up. We all make mistakes. Fortunately, I'd guess you have enough tokens to get through this without too much of an issue," Blake said.

"Tokens?" Kate asked.

"Yes. Let me tell you how Managing Your Tokens can help you out, time and time again."

Keeping Track of Tokens

Ellen Marcus was heading up a fledgling team at International Fragrance, overseeing a critical new project. The company's stock was down and her team's new initiative—a new line of scents for a large consumer products company—could mean a fat new contract for the company. The stakes were high, and Ellen had hired Blake to ensure that the team performed at its highest ability without wasting critical time.

The team had been assembled carefully, pulling the best talent from production, product development, marketing, and sales. It was the day of the first meeting, and everyone was gathered around the conference table, a bit nervous, but excited at the challenge that lay ahead of them.

"I'm so pleased that we have such an accomplished team," said Ellen. "We're going to go over the project objectives and then we'll discuss each team member's role in the project."

As they reviewed the roles, it became clear that the early pressure would be on the product development team members, who would need to develop samples on a tight deadline. It was decided that two product development team members would spearhead the efforts—John, a brilliant scientist known for his creative solutions and soft-spoken style, and Amy, a smart, ambitious junior member of the department with a very outgoing personality and equally brilliant although less refined solutions.

"Okay, everybody. To conclude, we'll meet again next Friday, so Amy can present the progress update for production," Ellen said. She turned to John. "I assume that's okay with you, John? I mean we want to be able to *hear* the update."

Ellen's joke made the team laugh as the meeting concluded. John, however, looked stricken as he left the room.

Blake had watched the situation closely. After everyone left the room, he approached Ellen.

"Ellen, I think you need to go get your token back," he said.

"Excuse me?"

"Your joke about John. Did you notice it seems to have caused some hurt feelings? Unless you want the initial efforts on this project stalled, I suggest you go make amends."

"Oh, you've got to be kidding, Blake! We're all big boys and girls here. Everyone knows John's got a thing about presenting in groups. I didn't say anything he wouldn't have said himself," she replied.

"Ellen, I think you need to understand a thing or two about Managing Your Tokens," Blake said, "and it all starts with understanding what I call 'your token account.'"

Your Token Account

We all have complex relationships in our work and home environments. We all have roles we play, and we all rely on others for key aspects of our success. Sometimes it's subordinates whose support we need to be ready to present to the group. Sometimes we need feedback and partnership from peers. Sometimes it's our boss from whom we need support. Other times it's friends, neighbors, or our partners and family.

In these relationships, colleagues, supervisors, family members, and others place a measure of trust in us. It's this trust that allows the relationship to exist and flourish. Yet every once in a while in business, as well as at home, each of us will slight, offend, or embarrass someone else, often another team member, in the normal course of doing our jobs. It's often quite accidental, and sometimes it's the result of passion for a project's outcome. At other times, we're irritable or distracted and snap at someone instead of using our more highly developed communication skills. In other situations, we must publicly disagree, which can appear to be a slight.

Our reputations are fairly fragile, and when it comes to interacting with people, we only get so many missteps in which we upset or embarrass the other party before they lose trust and faith in us and begin to shut down any and sometimes all interactions.

Imagine your reputation as a collaborative, effective and trusted team member represented by a small bag of three coins, or tokens. When you slight someone, those tokens begin to disappear. In the token economy, every time you offend or embarrass someone—whether accidentally or deliberately—they take a token from your bag. It doesn't matter whether you meant to deliver the slight or not; such actions always conclude with the loss of one of your tokens.

It only take a few of these situations before the your reputation begins to be tarnished within the group, causing labels such as "difficult," "rude," "untrustworthy," or "impossible" to be applied. These labels, whether true or not, clearly affect your ability to get things done as part of a team. If you're to remain a vital, respected member of the team, you must get these tokens back. The good news is, oftentimes you can.

Perhaps you're thinking, *Get it back? But that guy really deserved to be dressed down or thrown under the bus.*

That may be true. However, it's almost never a good idea to try to solve a conflict by creating a greater conflict. Teams need positive and open communication to work together effectively. By keeping track of your tokens and retrieving them when necessary, you show that you're someone who cares about relationships. Without that emphasis on relationships, your team will be less efficient and motivated, and a reputation as someone who has many damaged relationships can hurt your future opportunities. Colleagues may be less likely to refer you for jobs or pass along useful information. At the same time, those who are known for treating others with respect and fairness build trust and motivate others to help and support them.

Getting Your Token Back

A token can often be retrieved through an apology or an open, honest discussion of the situation in which it was lost. This is usually best done by approaching the offended party in private and offering a sincere apology. It's almost never a good idea to try to get your token back in public because it puts the person who was slighted in an awkward position. As part of the apology, it may also be appropriate to offer an explanation of the action, especially if it was done unintentionally. If the slight was intentional, it may be best to discuss the situation and find common ground for understanding and forgiveness.

However, no lost token is retrieved whole. When your conflict counterpart gives your token back to you, he or she keeps a little piece of it. You may be forgiven, but it can be hard to wholly win back the trust of the person you offended. Even if the other person wants to trust you again, he or she can't forget what happened "just like that."

That's why you can't disregard the importance of keeping your tokens in the first place. You can't pass a token around indefinitely because little pieces break off on each recovery. As time goes by, the number of tokens you have left, or pieces of tokens, represent your reputation.

Retrieving your tokens also depends on the person with whom you're engaging. Some people will make you seemingly beg for your token before giving it back, and others will hold grudges and never give it back at all. It may be that the slight or behavior was too grave. Or it could be that the person's perception of the slight or behavior is shaped by an experience that elevates its gravity for them.

For example, one young executive joked about killing herself if she had to do another boring project. This common if coarse statement was highly insulting to a co-worker with a close relative who had committed suicide. Joking about such a tragedy, even in the spirit of humorous exaggeration, made it unforgivable to her. Even a sincere apology couldn't retrieve the token in this case.

However, if you always try to get your token back, you will be operating from a much stronger position, since people will know you as someone who doesn't dole out offenses lightly. But that doesn't mean you need to grovel. There may be times when someone is particularly difficult or unreasonable about returning your token. Perhaps you've sincerely apologized and made a good faith effort to restore the relationship, but the offense is used as a weapon against you or held over your head. In such cases, it's not worth it to repeatedly try to get the token back. However, it's usually a good idea to try. If you forego token retrieval because it's unpleasant or because you've convinced yourself that you won't get it back anyway, then you've given up before you've tried.

Most of all, the effort to retrieve the token must be genuine. If you're acting disingenuously, you'll not only get less of the token back, you'll lose even more respect. That loss of respect can lead to being left out of meetings or being passed over for promotions or projects. Losing the goodwill that you have with the people around you and ignoring the consequences can be truly damaging to your career.

When you're a member of a team, especially in a leadership role (this can mean any form of leader, not just the manager or formal team leader), you need to care what others experience in working with and around you. When you don't care and give up all your tokens by being callous or overly direct or by ignoring others' feelings, people will ultimately stop following you. They may act in accordance with the requirements of their jobs and accept you as a supervisor, but they will do so with much less diligence and energy, reducing the productivity they would have in an environment in which they felt truly valued.

Kate's Token

When Blake finished explaining the concept of tokens, Kate was beaming with excitement.

"I definitely spent my tokens in this case—I broke my word to a manager, and I treated Carrie unfairly. But I know exactly what to do to get them back," she said.

"It happens to all of us sometimes. The key is to try to get the tokens back."

"Should you always try to get them back?" Kate asked.

"No. But in nearly all cases you should. People generally appreciate the effort and will give you at least part of a token back. In Ellen's case, she approached John, apologized for her insensitive remark, and offered him the opportunity to speak. He declined, but he appreciated her openness and the fact that she cared about his feelings. Their relationship improved because he realized how much she really cared about his input and experience."

"And what about when you're the person who gets tossed under the bus? Do you always have to give back the token?"

"Generally yes, but it's not always possible," said Blake. "There are some relatively rare situations where the offense is too intentional or too grave to be overcome by a simple apology. Instead, trust has to be won back by a long period of action that proves the person is sincere in making amends, and sometimes even that isn't enough. However, in most cases, even if you can't entirely forgive the person for a slight, it's a good idea to work toward moving past an unpleasant or upsetting incident if you wish to excel in your current work environment. Bad feelings and harbored resentment don't do anyone much good."

"Well, thanks, Blake." Kate said. "I've got to go. I clearly have a couple of tokens I've got to retrieve."

Chapter 5

EATING CRICKETS

Blake was loading his golf clubs into the car, getting ready to hit a bucket of balls, when his mobile phone rang. He saw that it was Kate.

"Hi, Kate."

"Hey, Blake. Got a minute?"

Blake looked at his golf clubs and smiled. He'd have to practice his swing another day.

"Sure. What can I do for you?"

"I'm livid. You remember David, the young guy on my team who's been doing such a stellar job? Well, I offered him that project leader opportunity and he turned it down. Can you believe it? This was such a plum opportunity for him."

"Did he say why?"

"No. That's just it! He didn't even have a good reason!"

"Well, Kate. There's almost always a good reason for these things, even if we don't know it. Sounds like he decided to Eat the Cricket on this one."

"What? Eww. Who would eat a cricket?"

Blake laughed a little, "Fair response, but let me tell you a story that might make you think about it a little differently."

Harrison's Choice

Harrison Green was a dynamic young MBA who was making great strides in his company. Recruited directly from New York University, he was fast becoming known for his creativity and problem-solving acumen. His ability to achieve in-depth knowledge of most of the product lines was uncanny. Nothing ruffled him, and his fellow employees and supervisors had great respect for him.

But despite his skill and success, Harrison's true passion wasn't his day job. He was an avid gardener and worked with a community garden that focused on youth involvement, providing healthful after-school activities and leadership training for young people. He never felt more joyful than when he was working in the dirt, helping kids who might otherwise be getting into trouble. Harrison didn't share this part of his life with many people—it was just something he did on his own time. He didn't consider it newsworthy.

At the office, Harrison was on a short-list of emerging leaders. When a new opportunity developed, his supervisor, Andrea, thought it was a perfect match for his skill set, and she called him into a meeting to discuss the opportunity.

"Harrison, we have a fantastic new opportunity opening and leading a new facility that will become the company's new hub of customer service. It's a very high-profile position, and we'd like to offer it to you. You'd be managing more than one hundred people, be the site director, and likely double your salary. As you make this a success, it's going to mean a long, bright future at this company," said Andrea, beaming.

Harrison had to catch his breath for a moment. He hadn't been expecting such a big jump so soon. He thought of how he would be able to move out of his tiny apartment and donate more money to the community garden. This was turning out to be a great day. And a seat at the leadership table was a great change-up here at work.

"Sounds very exciting. When do I start," he asked with a smile.

"Well, there's one other factor. The new facility is in Hyderabad, India," Andrea responded. "I hope that won't make a difference in your decision."

Harrison's face fell. Move to India? That would mean leaving his life here. All his friends, his family, and it dawned on him—his garden community.

"In India? There's no way to do the job from here?"

"No. The new facility is in India."

"Well, how long do you expect I would need to be there?" he asked.

"It's hard to say. It would be at least two or three years. Maybe five, depending on how things go. But you would be able to transfer back after five years if you chose to do so," Andrea explained.

Five years. By the time he got back, even the youngest members of the community garden would have graduated from high school, and he would have missed all of their commencements. The garden wasn't quite to the point where it could sustain itself and hire a full-time director. Who would see it through to that point?

At the same time, all of his hard work at his job was paying off in the most unexpected fashion—he would be the youngest manager in the history of the company to have so much responsibility.

Harrison studied the edge of the table, unsure of what to say. On paper, this was his dream job, except for the move to India.

Andrea shifted uncomfortably.

"This wasn't exactly the response I was expecting, Harrison. You're young and dynamic. You've worked so hard to get here. What's the problem?"

"Problem?" he said, looking up. "It's not really a problem. It's just a lot to take in so quickly. The job sounds fantastic. I just hadn't considered moving away, certainly not so far away. Give me a little time to consider all this." He stood to leave.

"I hope you understand that this is a chance nobody would pass up," Andrea emphasized. "You're going to learn a lot from it and really prove out all the education and hard work you've put into your career so far. You'll be great in this role."

As he left Andrea's office Harrison said quietly to himself, "Yeah. I think this is a chance of a lifetime. I just have to figure out how to make the move."

Harrison spent a restless night contemplating his options. He had an ongoing internal disagreement about what he thought he should do versus what he really knew was best for him. Finally, in the early morning hours, he reached a decision. It was one that immediately brought him peace. The next morning, he went looking for Andrea and found her in her office.

"Andrea, you have a minute?"

"Certainly Harrison; come on in."

"First, I have to say I am so flattered by your confidence in me. I know it's a bit of a gamble to invest so quickly in a guy with my experience. But I've decided to decline the Hyderabad offer. In fact, I'm going to be submitting an application to the work-share program and reduce my hours here to half-time."

"What?" Andrea's face showed her shock.

"Yes, as soon as that goes into effect, I'm going to take a position as the Allendale Community Garden's first executive director."

The previous evening, while he was struggling with the decision, Harrison had spoken to a few of his closest friends and family members. They were all excited at the offer. They were disappointed that he'd be moving away for a while, but they knew the role would bring him back to the main office quite frequently and that he'd be back permanently in just a couple of years, likely as a vice president. The strange thing was that none of them seemed to really understand how hard it would be for him to leave the Allendale project.

It took hours of thinking, but Harrison eventually realized that he wanted the Allendale team more than this new job. He essentially chose to Eat the Cricket.

Blake paused for a moment to allow Kate to take in what he'd said.

Then he continued, "Kate, what would you eat if you wanted an excellent source of nutrition, something high in protein and low in fat? Something easy to harvest that wouldn't damage the environment?" He waited.

"You mean crickets," Kate responded. "But I'm not sure I could do that, Blake, no matter what the preparation method."

"That's the point, Kate. Many people are repulsed by the thought of eating a cricket, but that doesn't mean, when you think about it, that it's the wrong choice. And who said crickets are bad anyway?"

Bucking Conventional Wisdom

Decades of cultural programming make it difficult for us to see or take hold of opportunities that are right in front of us. We can find ourselves reluctant to make the obvious choice because of a deeper desire for a different option that is more "palatable" by traditional standards and norms.

Think of this reluctance to do what is objectively the right thing to do as the conflict between your true desires and the proverbial mother who is guiding you as you reach a crossroads. When you have an important decision to make, your internal conditioning often kicks in, guiding you according to the norms with which you have been brought up and are comfortable.

In Harrison's case, the mother is screaming, "You got your MBA! You have student loans to pay! You've worked so hard to get to this position! Why would you throw it all away?"

But often, those norms can lead us down what's the wrong path for us, a path of comfortable expectation rather than innovation and opportunity based on who we are as individuals. This is an important concept for both teams and individuals. Are we making choices because they're safe, familiar, and expected? Or are we taking a look at the opportunities ahead of us, properly considering cultural or other biases, and objectively evaluating our opportunities?

If we're doing the latter, we may sometimes find ourselves Eating the Cricket, but then we find that doing so isn't as bad as we thought it would be. The fact is, you don't want to be a person who mindlessly follows society's expectations. You want to think for yourself, decide for yourself.

The cricket analogy plays out often in our professional and personal lives. It might be found in pursuing a job you love that goes against gender norms, or when a colleague gives up an opportunity in order to protect other priorities. Nonetheless, even when the benefits of making the change are clear logically, the process of going against cultural norms can make the opportunity so unpalatable as to take it out of consideration before it's ever in the running—like the thought of Eating the Cricket.

For teams, this can be dangerous. Team members who are inhibited by corporate culture may dismiss opportunities because it's not "how it's done" at their company. However, by making team members aware of crickets, we can empower them to look past cultural biases against certain ideas or processes, which means new opportunities can emerge that are right for them as individuals.

Taking on an unpopular role—especially a role that others might not respect but that could be a great learning experience—can be challenging, even if it's something you would enjoy doing. In many companies, getting great people into roles like this is affected in no small part by crickets. Some tend to look down on these roles as not "valuable" or "important." People don't want these roles because of perceptions, not because of what they really have to offer. At times, breaking from the pack and choosing to take one of these roles is really the best choice - as is Eating the Crickets. In many companies, the roles in customer support are considered 'less than' roles that produce the product. But, at a particular stage in your career, you might benefit from learning how to really connect with and deliver superior support to customers. This is not an easy skill, as anyone in this role can attest.

Considering the Cricket

"So, you're saying that David is going to leave and go join a gardening commune somewhere?"

Blake laughed. "No, not exactly. But he seems to have determined that the right decision for him is something else. Something he's apparently not comfortable sharing with you."

"Well, I suppose that could be true. How do we know when it's the right time to—and I can't believe I'm saying this—Eat the Cricket?"

"Well, you have to decide what's right for you and ignore the cultural norms. Is that inner voice your true passion, or is it pressuring you to avoid doing the right thing because other people may find it distasteful or unconventional?"

"Hmm. Should we always Eat the Cricket?"

"No, that's not the point. Sometimes you might choose to, but in other cases you might find that for good reasons, taking the path that social norms suggest is the right choice for you at that time. Harrison could have chosen to go to Hyderabad and used the expanded funds he'd be earning to help the gardening society from afar, until he returned home. This would have been a valid choice, if he himself had chosen it."

"Clearly, I need to go speak with David," Kate concluded. "I mean, I'd really like to know what his choice was, and to let him know he's got my support, even if it means we Eat the Cricket together."

After a short pause, Kate offered, "I guess we all fall victim to blindly avoiding the crickets every once in a while. But Blake?"

"Yes, Kate?"

"Please don't ever try to make me eat a real cricket."

Chapter 6

DIGGING THE PERFECT HOLE IN THE WRONG PLACE

Blake, waiting at the corner coffee shop, looked at his watch. Kate was nearly twenty-five minutes late. He was mildly worried, since she prided herself on punctuality. Then he looked out the window and saw her hurrying across the street.

She rushed through the doors and to the table where he sat, plopping down in the chair across from him.

"Hi. Sorry I'm so late. I was working on this big project and overslept, then my cell phone died . . ." She stopped to take a breath.

"It's fine. Are you okay? You seem a little overwhelmed."

"Yes, I'm fine. But I've been spending a lot of time working on a new idea for my division. I read this story in *The Wall Street Journal* about the explosion in new media companies overseas and I thought it would be a good idea to expand our practice to include that area."

Blake took a sip of his coffee and considered her statement for a moment.

"And how did that go?" he asked.

"Well, as I was explaining my ideas in the team meeting, my boss pointed out a memo that was reviewed at last month's meeting—the one I completely missed because I was working from home that day on this new stuff. All I could say was, 'Memo?' I didn't even know about the team meeting. He didn't seem too pleased."

"So, what did that memo cover?" Blake asked.

"Well, only that the company has tightened its focus to domestic consulting for the coming fiscal year. To me, it seems a bit restrictive, especially given the idea I've been fleshing out."

"Well, you might want to go back and take a look at that memo before you do any more work on your idea."

"I don't think I'll be doing more work on the idea at all," Kate replied. "My boss and I talked more after the meeting and now I realize I've wasted a lot of time. I should have asked him about it first, but I thought he'd be impressed with my initiative if I pursued it without his knowledge. Now I just feel silly."

"Don't feel silly," Blake responded. "Most people don't catch on as quickly as you did, and they continue to charge forward with their ideas in spite of the fact that they're not in line with the company's objectives. I came across a revealing expression when I was working with an employee at a local beverage company down south. It's where I first encountered the problem of Digging the Perfect Hole in the Wrong Place."

Kate settled into her chair.

"I'm all ears."

Digging the Perfect Hole

For the past three months, Rick Jensen had been working on a research report based on an idea he'd developed for his department. As part of a product development team for a beverage company, he was looking for a way to make himself stand out to his supervisors.

After tasting some particularly flavorful vitamin water, Rick was convinced his company should get into the vitamin water and enhanced beverage market. He authorized a small study and, without his teams consent, spent a portion of the team's discretionary budget. He knew he was taking a risk by doing so, but he was willing to bet his team members would be so impressed by the potential and the product ideas that ultimately they wouldn't mind. Better in this case, he reasoned, to ask forgiveness than to ask permission.

The day he hit "send" on the research report, distributing the 150-page document to his entire team, his supervisor, and his supervisor's supervisor, he felt a bit giddy. Finally, his team members, some of whom had been complaining about his lack of availability and general performance lately, would see all his hard work. They'd understand that he had a bigger agenda that would benefit all of them.

Later that afternoon, Rick hadn't heard anything from his team members. He went to the break room to grab a snack and saw Fred, his supervisor, and Sandra, one of the team members, sitting at one of the tables. They stopped talking when he walked into the room.

"Hey, guys. I'm glad you're here. Did you get my email earlier today?" he asked.

Sandra looked at Fred, then rose from her seat and said, "Uh, yeah. But I'm really late for a conference call. I'll catch up with you later." She walked quickly out of the room.

A bit puzzled, Rick turned to Fred. "So? What did you think?"

"Look, Rick. I think we should talk about this later. It's not the time."

"What do you mean? Is there something wrong?" Rick realized that Fred didn't seem excited about the report.

"Well, yes. You've been late on your project milestones for a few months now. I've been covering for you because I figured you had something personal going on. But now I see that you've been spending time and company resources on a project that really isn't part of our team's goals for this year," Fred said.

Rick was stunned. "But Fred. This is a huge opportunity. Didn't you read the report?"

"Yes, I read it. But what you didn't read was our company's annual report, which outlines how we're going to stay focused on our core business units and cut back on new product development. Listen," Fred explained, "you did solid work, but this is a project that won't fly right now. If this were last year, you'd have a potential homerun here. But you should have talked to me about it before you invested so much valuable time. Today, we just won't make investments like this."

Understanding Where to Dig

Rick is guilty of Digging the Perfect Hole in the Wrong Place. He tackled the research well. He produced a solid proposal backed by independent research. However, his efforts were wasted because it was something the company couldn't consider at this point in its operations. He allowed his passion for an idea to distract him from evaluating the value of the proposal and the probability of the company embracing the idea and its potential outcome at this particular time.

There are many costs associated with Digging the Perfect Hole in the Wrong Place and three key points to consider before you begin. First is the simple waste of time and resources when you fail to dig in the right place. Progress on your company's main projects is slowed and real dollars are sometimes spent and wasted.

Second, in addition to this waste of time and money, Rick likely damaged his reputation with his co-workers and his supervisors.

His co-workers might wonder why he didn't trust them enough to share what he was doing with them, raising a number of other questions. Why was he hiding this big project? Why wouldn't he share it with the team and get their input? How dare he tap resources that were earmarked for the team's success and use them at his own discretion? It might look like Rick was trying to make a name for himself at the expense of his team members. This is likely what caused Sandra to exit the break room so quickly.

Finally, because he spent company time and resources on a project destined to go nowhere, his managers may begin to question his judgment. They may be annoyed that he's devoted time to something other than the most important team tasks. They may also wonder how he missed the fact that his pet project was so out of line with the greater company mission. This could cause longer-term damage to his career prospects.

These common downsides to digging in the wrong place show us just some of what can go wrong when we don't pay attention to where we're digging.

Why Would Anyone Dig in the Wrong Place?

We all "dig" in our jobs. We focus on and try to deliver great solutions, innovative ideas, and quality follow-through for the tasks we perform. In short, we want to deliver by digging the perfect hole. Digging the Perfect Hole in the Wrong Place, however, is usually a result of passion that forgot to look at the company goals, as was the case with Rick. He produced quality work that was out of line with the company's needs.

That's not to say that passion and conviction aren't important. They are. However, ultimately, the company decides whether the "hole"—the output, the project, the product itself—has been dug in the right place.

That simply means that, because the organization is paying for the hole, its managers decide whether such output is in alignment with the overall vision, mission, and desired outcomes of the company.

Therefore, it's important to align individual passion with organizational objectives to ensure that your individual or team efforts are not only those you believe to be right but are supported and valued by the organization.

As much as it defies conventional wisdom, there are times when passion can actually get in the way of your success, especially when it blinds you to reality. Your passion may lead you to believe that others in the company don't understand what's best when determining what projects to invest in and when. Like Rick, it may seem like a better idea to dig the hole where you think it should go. Then, the reasoning goes, everyone will realize that you were right all along. But this holds a lot of risks, including the risk of digging in the wrong place and not realizing it.

The big punch line is that it often takes the same amount of effort— and sometimes less effort because of the support that is provided—to dig the hole in the right place than it does to dig it in the wrong place. You can toil and dig until you dig the hole of your dreams, but unless you're clearly communicating and ensuring that your vision and values are in alignment with the bigger picture, you could find that your efforts have been egregiously misplaced and won't be valued in the end.

The fact is, companies would prefer a "rough chip" in the right place over a perfect hole in the wrong place. Think about it. A rough chip in the right place could be expanded and perfected by Rick and others on the team. A perfect hole in the wrong place represents not only wasted effort and resources but the opportunity costs, or what could have been accomplished if efforts had been directed in the right place. Sometimes, those misplaced efforts also have direct costs because we have to spend time refilling the hole created by misdirected efforts.

To correct the situation, Rick needs to make amends with his team and redirect his efforts so they pay off for everyone involved. He also needs to modify his approach to new projects going forward. First, he should always ask himself, "Are my efforts aligned with stated business goals?" Second, he should frequently validate his direction and approach with his manager and other key people. Sharing and validating can be a powerful way to strengthen your efforts when done properly. And clearly, not doing so can have perilous risks to those of us digging the hole.

What to Consider Before You Start to Dig

Consider three aspects before you start to dig. First, how much value is being brought by the work output? For example, is it consistent with the company's overall goals and therefore valuable to the company?

Second, how well done is the work? If the work is valuable but sloppily done, the value is diminished compared to a well-executed job.

Finally, how much effort is required to complete the work? The key challenge these answers reveal is that individuals often unconsciously think of the rewards and compensation for the projects they deliver will be determined first on the "Effort Required", second the "Quality of Work", and lastly the "Value to the Company." People too often feel they should earn big bonuses because they've worked hard instead of looking at the value or quality of the work delivered.

Performing companies, on the other hand, evaluate employee results and deliverables in this order: "Value to the Company," "Quality of Work," and "Effort Required." Notice the difference in priorities? Yes, companies routinely recognize effort with bonuses and other rewards, but not efforts that don't deliver value to the company. Armed with this view, it becomes clear that in order to be successful over time, we really need to align our evaluation of our work in this order. We need to make sure we're always digging in the right place first (value), and then make it the perfect hole (quality). That shows the management team that we "get it" and can be trusted to devote our efforts to the overall strategies and objectives of the company, thereby delivering more value throughout the organization.

Blake's Take

"So, I'm Rick," Kate said with a sheepish grin.

"Well, the situations are similar," Blake concurred. "But we all make this mistake from time to time. It happens when we're out of alignment with the bigger picture of our circumstances. The difference is that you were smart enough to catch yourself and not forge on because you couldn't admit you'd dug the hole in the wrong place."

"But what about when you do have a new idea that could be a breakthrough?" Kate argued. "It might never be recognized if you don't break out of old ideas and paradigms."

"That's a good point. It comes down to a matter of impact. You have to show that your ideas and efforts will produce an impact that is important to the company or else the hole needs to be dug elsewhere, even if you don't agree."

Blake added, "I would never suggest you don't make big bets and gamble a bit with pushing the envelope. You should. However, if you do it right, you're thinking first and foremost about "where to dig" more than you are about perfection. Or worse, trying to pretend that what you can or desire to dig is what the company should need or want."

Kate nodded.

"Early in my career," Blake continued, "I worked with a woman named Isabella. We had very similar skill sets and strengths and soon a friendly competition emerged. We each worked on high-profile projects. To make myself stand apart, I worked many extra hours, ensuring that all my reports were immaculately designed and formatted. I was at my desk nights and weekends poring over each report, choosing spacing, fonts, and graphics. The presentations were truly stunning if I do say so myself."

"Graphics?"

Blake smiled. "Well, I thought they were important, but I learned my supervisors didn't agree. Isabella got promoted first. At first I was angry. I was the one working nights and weekends. I thought I clearly deserved the promotion more. It wasn't until my supervisor explained to me that by spending so much time on something that really wasn't that important, I was actually hurting myself. I was the guy who could make things look good, but I was spending too much time on each report. I wasn't spending time doing something the company valued, which was thinking through the ideas and consequences within the reports. Isabella was more focused and in tune with the company's value structure and she was rightly rewarded with the promotion ahead of me. The tough part of the lesson was that if I had just asked my supervisor, he'd have made it very clear where I should have been focusing my efforts.

"It was the last time I made such a mistake," Blake continued. "Now it's my priority to always check and double-check that the time and effort I'm expending are in the best interests of the company. And that is almost never a solo proposition. I don't want to be Digging a Perfect Hole in the Wrong Place ever again."

"But isn't it the manager's job to make sure their team is digging in the right place?" Kate asked.

"Sure, but managers can't direct you if they don't know what you're doing. In your case and in Rick's case, the efforts were done without the manager's knowledge," Blake reminded her. "And let's face it—none of us want our managers constantly checking up on us. We want the autonomy to be professional and do our jobs. That comes with the responsibility to own where we're digging and to get the proper information and feedback to make sure the hole placement is on target.

While managers need to check in with their team members periodically and give clear guidance, it's also our responsibility to pay attention and really act on this input. At the same time, when people are frustrated with their reviews, it's usually because they're not respecting that where they put the hole isn't valued and they're expecting to be rewarded for effort, regardless of value to the company or team."

Kate considered this for a moment.

"It does make sense that success lies in value, quality, and effort—those are key factors for the overall success of any team or company. I guess I'd better make sure I'm looking at my efforts the same way the company is," she said, then added with a sheepish grin, "And not miss any more of those team meetings."

Chapter 7

DOING A TEN POUND JOB

Blake walked onto the racquetball court where Kate was already warming up. She had a fierce backhand that usually bested him. Today, she seemed to be hitting the ball particularly hard and it sailed by him, narrowly missing his shoulder.

"Sorry about that. I didn't see you come in," Kate said.

"I almost feel sorry for the ball. Something wrong?" Blake asked.

"Nah. It's just performance review time. Most of my team has been doing wonderfully, but there's one team member who does a good job but does too much of everything, and it's becoming a problem."

"What do you mean, 'too much of everything?'" Blake asked.

"Well, when I ask her for a report, she does a great job, but she gives me fifteen pages of documentation when two or three would do. When she takes on a project, the research portion takes her an extra few weeks because she over-analyzes everything. It slows her up and makes my job harder than it needs to be. She just overdoes everything," Kate replied.

"Sounds like she's putting eleven pounds in every ten-pound bag," he said. Kate paused. "Analogy?"

Blake smiled. "Absolutely."

Kate motioned to the door. "How about we take a break before we even start this game?"

An Eleven-Pound Problem

Carl and Ellen Paradise, a husband-and-wife team, owned Paradise Design, an advertising agency that handled almost all the print advertising and collateral development for FunTime Parks, a national chain of amusement parks.

Carl and Ellen were beginning to worry about the FunTime account. They sensed that things might not be going well, but they couldn't quite understand why. Their team always produced more concepts than was required. If the client wanted a few campaign ideas, Carl and Ellen came back with at least a dozen. It was always their goal to make sure the client had enough options to get exactly what they needed. The client had called a meeting to discuss the future of the account and the Paradises were worried. This was their biggest account.

When Carl and Ellen got to the meeting, they were visibly nervous. After pleasantries were exchanged in the conference room, there was a moment of silence, since no one wanted to bridge the unpleasant topic first. Keith Hartson, FunTime's marketing director, finally broke the tension.

"We're concerned because turnaround time on most projects is too long," he said. "We're getting a dozen ideas for every initiative when what we really need are two or three of your best. What's frustrating is that this isn't the first time we've asked. In our last planning meeting, I said it wasn't necessary to provide so many concepts. Getting consensus and approvals on such varied design options is almost impossible," he explained.

Carl looked shocked. He couldn't believe the client was unhappy because his agency over-delivered. He could only manage a quiet, "I see."

"You've been a good partner and get excellent results," said Keith. "But aside from the time it takes to wade through all the design options, my boss questions whether this is a way of padding your bills. I know that's not the case. Your rates are very fair. But I feel like you're not listening to what we need."

"So, you're saying you want less work from us?" Ellen asked.

"Not necessarily less work, but I want you to take a firm stand on what you believe we should do. We can be much more effective and fast-moving if we have two or three concepts backed by solid research and your expertise than if we have a dozen ideas without context. More depth, less quantity," he explained.

Understanding the Concept of the Ten-Pound Job

Imagine a flood-threatened community where local citizens are working to stave off rising waters using bags of sand. It was established that each bag needs ten pounds of sand—no more, no less. Fill the bags too full, and the sand eventually runs out. Why? All the bags eventually break open because they're filled beyond their capacity.

Fill them with only nine pounds of sand and its likely there won't be enough bags to hold all the sand available. Besides, underfilled bags won't fit together into a strong wall and will eventually collapse as the water grows higher.

Filling the Ten-Pound Bag with ten-pounds of sand means doing the right job rather than over- or under-delivering on expectations and real needs. Over and under delivering can both have devastating effects.

If you've over-delivered from the beginning, you might find you don't have the energy or time to complete the tasks at hand and you might have to cut corners to finish the project. If you're under-delivering, you may get the project done, but with sub-standard quality or insufficient work, either of which could contribute to the failure of the entire project.

It's easy for most of us to assume that more is better, as the Paradise team did, but consistent over-performance will lead to inefficient teams and team members. A team or individual who spends too much energy overdoing it, even in the right place, incurs lost opportunity costs because they don't have the resources to capitalize on new opportunities that might arise. It's bad enough when one person's efforts aren't in synch with what is actually required. When this spreads across the entire team, the impact is multiplied exponentially. Whether you're a team member or a manager, it's essential to ensure that fellow members are creating value in proportion to the potential pay-off of the project.

While it may have seemed like a good idea for the Paradise team to bring multiple design concepts to every project, this is actually an example of doing an eleven-pound job. It was costing the agency time it could have devoted to other billable work while not actually adding value to the project, and in this case it clearly alienated the client. Overall, predictably it was an ineffective strategy, even though it may have seemed, on the surface, like great client service.

In the meeting, Ellen turned to Keith and said, "When you initially asked us to bring in fewer designs, we thought you were just concerned about our time; that you were being nice and looking out for us. We had no idea it was really a problem for you. I'm so sorry about that, Keith."

Keith looked a little relieved. "I couldn't get into all the specifics about it, but it was frustrating when I kept getting multiple designs for everything. It really slows things down on our end. But I suppose I could have been more direct about what I was asking."

"We really didn't realize this was a problem. We thought 'The more, the better.' It was just our way of trying to provide good customer service. But we'll definitely be more focused from now on," said Carl.

Courtside Consultation

"So," Blake concluded, "the problem could be that your employee doesn't realize that your requests for less work are related to making the team more effective overall. You may need to educate her about the opportunity cost of her actions, not to mention the impact on you."

Kate nodded. "Interesting. I remember when I was first starting out, I stayed long hours just to prove to my boss I was working hard, even though I usually finished my work in time to leave at 5:00. I didn't want him to think I was just a 'nine-to-fiver.' In hindsight, that was silly. He thought I was overwhelmed with my work and was actually ready to cut my responsibilities. Maybe my employee thinks this is the way to prove herself," said Kate.

"It's possible. You've also met those people who insist that everything has be done to perfection, always. But often, 'perfection' doesn't add to value—it just increases costs. The eleven pounder needs to learn when to deliver everything and when to say 'This is enough,'" Blake explained.

"Without being a nine-pound slacker."

"Not quite. Nine-pounders aren't necessarily 'under performing' in the classic sense. It can be more subtle than that. They can believe they're getting the job done, and sometimes yes, they are in fact trying to put in minimal effort to 'check off' the deliverable. But their output is so close to 'right' as to be undetectable while the work is going on. They clearly get how to do the work correctly, but they aren't," Blake explained.

"What do you do about them?"

"They need coaching to deliver the right output as well, or they need to be removed from their roles. But these people aren't the ones coming in late, playing games at work, and otherwise being clear slackers. Oftentimes the nine-pounder is too focused on getting the specific task done—filling all the bags—rather than the true mission of building an effective wall of sandbags."

While Kate thought about this, Blake added, "It's important to make them see their role in the big picture so they understand that their goal isn't just to fill the bags but to fill them properly and build a great and effective wall. Otherwise, they may think they're doing the right job when they aren't."

"But if they're slackers, what do you do?" Kate persisted.

"Well, you need training and performance reviews. Some nine-pounders and even eleven-pounders need to be removed from the team if they truly can't or won't change to adapt to the real deliverables and success goals of the game," said Blake.

"This has been helpful," Kate said. "I see now what I need to do with Jenny. Given her drive to make good things happen, I think a discussion about Filling the Ten-Pound Bag will provide clarity for her. Of course, now I'm thinking about who on the team might be doing this nine-pound game."

"Wait, speaking of the game, let's get back to me beating you here on the racquetball court, shall we?"

Kate grinned. "I'll take care of these matters back at the office in an hour."

Chapter 8

THE VIEW FROM THE CHEAP SEATS

I t's just silly," Kate fretted.

Blake looked at her as he set his bag down and asked, "What's that?"

"One of my former team members, Alison. She just got this great promotion offer to head up her own team—after I went to bat for her. And now I've just learned that she's leaving to go to the middle of nowhere and work on her family's farm. She's on such a fast track here. How could she give that up?'"

"Well, did she give any indication why she made this decision?"

"Not really. She said something about needing to head back home. It would have been nice if she'd gotten homesick before I spent so much time selling her to management," Kate complained. "Now I look like an idiot."

"Well, things are always easy when viewed from the Cheap Seats," Blake smiled.

"Hey! What do you mean by that? I've known this woman for three years! I've been helping her career and giving her advice. She's confided a great deal in me. I'm not exactly judging this with no information," Kate defended herself.

"Kate, whenever we're looking at and guiding someone else's situation, no matter how close or how far removed we are from them, we're always in the cheap seats," said Blake. "Do you want to hear why?"

Kate looked skeptical and said, "Okay. Convince me."

Frank's Dilemma

For more than a year, Frank Ashton had been analyzing the expansion opportunities for his employer, a large insurance firm, into the European and Asian markets. He approached his supervisor, Anderson Langley, and made a strong case for both—the numbers were right and it looked like the timing couldn't be better for the company, which was coming off of a very good year.

Anderson agreed and got Frank time with the board to review his findings and recommendations.

As he spoke to the board, Frank felt good. The presentation seemed to be going well, and he was certain they'd at least be willing to move forward with the European expansion and that they'd appoint him to oversee it.

Later that day, Frank entered Anderson's office with a grin that stretched from ear to ear, clearly expecting good news.

"So, let's hear it," he said.

Anderson asked Frank to sit down. He carefully explained that the expansion was postponed, leaving out some of the CFO's concerns because they were still considered confidential.

Frank's face reddened as he realized his hard work would not result in the outcome he'd anticipated.

"So, you're saying that the past year of work was a waste of time?" he asked.

"No, of course not," Anderson replied. "The board just decided that the timing wasn't right for the company, but they're going to revisit it again at the start of the next fiscal year."

"That's eleven months away," Frank objected. "We were supposed to present at the start of this fiscal year so that we could get it done this year."

"I'm really sorry, Frank. We were all hoping this would be a go ASAP," said Anderson.

"Well, I guess there's nothing else to say." Frank rose and left the office, clearly disappointed.

After work, he met his best friends, Rob and Ted, for a drink at a local restaurant.

Rob, who had listened to Frank's excitement over the expansion for months, was outraged on Frank's behalf.

"You should quit. Seriously, man. They don't deserve you and they don't appreciate you," he said, then took a sip of his beer.

"Quit? I can't quit. We have two kids. What about the mortgage?" Frank looked defeated.

Ted, who worked with Frank, agreed with Rob. "What's it going to look like to your employees? You need to get out of there. Make a bold move. Show them they can't treat you like this. Plus, they're not going to really let you go. They'll counter-offer. I guarantee it."

Frank thought over his friends' advice as he drove home. It would feel good to walk into the office the next day and hand over his resignation. They would be shocked. And Ted was probably right. They might even reconsider the expansion to keep him.

By the time he discussed the situation with his wife that night, Frank had begun to seriously toy with the idea of quitting. He ran the idea past Julie and she turned pale.

"Quitting? Really, Frank? I mean, I'll support you in whatever you want to do, but that seems like a rash move. And it would be tough for us to make it on my salary alone."

Julie looked worried, and Frank was mildly annoyed that she wasn't more enthusiastic. He repeated Ted's words about how the company would likely counter and would never let him go because he was too valuable.

Later, the thought of the shock on Anderson's face if he handed him a letter of resignation helped him drift off to sleep.

Who Sits in the Cheap Seats?

When we're faced with decisions and setbacks in our lives, there are usually plenty of people around willing to give advice. They may be spouses, friends, relatives, mentors, or even just casual acquaintances. They may be concerned for us and have a vested interest in our well-being, or they may have random opinions based on what they think they might do in such a situation.

When faced with important decisions or issues, many of these people may believe they are as affected by the circumstances as you are or feel the impact as much as you do, but they aren't and they don't. Even those who are closest to us are in the cheap seats of many aspects of these types of situations. They're not on the floor; they're not actually playing the game. Rather, they're watching from the sidelines, coaching us and providing direction, much as excited fans do during a ball game—from the cheap seats.

There are a few problems associated with blindly following the advice of people in the cheap seats. Everyone who is giving you advice, from your spouse to your parents to your boss to your best friend, is biased in some way. They may be focusing on the impact of your decision on them and trying to influence it. They may just want to see you change a situation that is making you unhappy without regard for the long-term consequences. They may even be living vicariously through you.

Even people who love us have biases, even if those biases are simply to see things play out in our best interests. Those offering advice or helping us explore options may not be emotionally invested in the situation—or, at least, not as emotionally invested as we are—or its outcomes. They can easily help us discover and evaluate the facts, but how we feel and what we want is quite individual and personal. They can't help here, which is what really puts them in the cheap seats to begin with.

Even armed with "the facts," we need to be mindful that they usually don't have all the information, even if we've shared as much as possible with them. It's similar to when a friend is in a bad romantic relationship. The friend confides in you whenever things are going poorly. After a while, you may say, "I don't know how you could possibly stay with that person," but the reality is that there's a great deal of good in the relationship. Since the friend only tells you the negative parts, your perception is skewed. Likewise, we often don't consider or accept that we don't see all the parts, and therefore we give advice based on a faulty understanding of the circumstances.

And of course, some seats are cheaper than others—or at least offer different views. Your spouse may be your confidant, but he or she isn't in the situation with you, understanding all the dynamics and feeling what you feel.

For example, in Frank's case, no one close to him was privy to the fact that a board meeting had been held right after his presentation in which concerns about the upcoming fiscal year were aired. Without that knowledge, the delay in approving the proposal looked callous and dismissive of Frank and his work, which is how Rob and Ted saw the situation.

However, since even Frank didn't know the whole picture, those close to him couldn't possibly counsel him knowledgeably.

Ironically, the board was in fact excited about the proposal and had every intention of implementing it—and placing Frank in charge of the expansion—in the next fiscal year.

There are still more potential issues with others' agendas, so look around and pay attention. What is this person's interest in giving you advice about this topic? In Frank's case, his wife was concerned for their family's well-being, while his supervisor didn't want to lose one of his best people.

In the case of Frank's friend and co-worker Ted, there may have been a professional motivation behind his urging Frank to resign. In some cases, professional ambition or jealousy can color the advice of friends and colleagues in a negative way. To wit, Frank leaving his post would open up a greater opportunity for Ted to move up in the company.

At other times, friends may feel a sense of bravado and enjoy the opportunity to live vicariously through your situation, which causes them to give you advice they themselves would never follow.

As it turns out, Rob and Ted were defensive on their friend's behalf, concerned for his feelings and the respect they thought he was due, but they were also acting from a sense of bravado—Rob had been through a similar circumstance the previous year and had quietly accepted it. This was indeed his opportunity to vicariously voice the anger he'd felt then. And Ted was mildly jealous of Frank. Though he'd never admit it, he knew Frank's absence would clear the way for new opportunities for him.

As Frank sat at his desk the next day, considering his options prior to meeting with Anderson, he was still unsure how he was going to proceed. He loved the company and had played a key role in developing the product. Many of his team members had become good friends over the years, and he would be reluctant to leave them. Some of them knew about his plan for expansion and were just as excited about it as he was.

And, of course, the uncertainty of the market left him fearful that he would be putting too much stress on his wife if he left the company.

He was still mulling over all these points when he got up from his desk to go to Anderson's office. His phone rang and he turned back to answer it. It was Rob.

"Did you tell them to get lost yet?" Rob joked.

"No. I'm meeting with Anderson in a few minutes," said Frank.

"Good. Tell him exactly what you think of their gutless ways. Remember, man. No guts, no glory." Rob hung up.

As Frank hung up, he felt a bit uncomfortable. Rob seemed a little too invested in his resignation—almost as though this was a game to him. That was mildly disturbing, but even after he arrived at Anderson's office, Frank still wasn't sure how the conversation would go. He sat on the opposite site of Anderson's polished mahogany desk and listened to what Anderson had to say.

"Frank, I understand that the board's decision is disappointing, but I want you to know that their decision had nothing to do with the quality of your report. Everyone agrees that you did excellent work and you've identified a significant opportunity for the company," he said.

With those words, Frank relaxed a bit. Although he hadn't admitted it to anyone, he'd been afraid he hadn't done as well on the report as he'd first thought and that perhaps had been the basis for the board's decision.

"I spoke with several of the members today and got permission to share some broad strokes of our plan," Anderson continued. "I realize that the way the decision was communicated to you might have left you with the wrong impression."

He explained that the company had some big-picture issues that had to be addressed in the immediate future. It was nothing that would directly affect Frank or his team, but it would tie up some of the human and capital resources that Frank would need if they were to proceed with the expansion. Since the expansion was so important for the future of the company, they wanted to wait until the next fiscal year when Frank would have the participation and capital he needed for success.

The grin that had been on Frank's face the day before returned. "So, you're saying that we're moving forward?"

Anderson grinned back. "Well, I can't say that on the record."

"And you're saying that I'll be your point person in Europe?"

"Can't tell you that on the record, either." Anderson's tone was all the assurance that Frank needed.

"Well, off the record, I can tell you that I won't let you down," said Frank, shaking Anderson's hand.

Kate's Colleague

"What you're saying is that I don't have all the facts about Alison. And maybe I'm a little too invested in the situation to be objective," Kate said.

"Well, invested and certainly not seeing the whole picture," Blake returned. "Is Alison homesick? Does she have a sick family member she needs to tend to? Are there financial or personal issues involved? Does she have a partner or family members who have weighed in and convinced her to take action? Maybe she doesn't value her career in this field as much as you do. Without these facts, we can't make assumptions about what is in her best interests," said Blake. "And, yes, your concern for your own reputation may be coloring your outlook just a bit."

Kate considered this a moment. "But I honestly don't feel jealous or angry. I really want what's best for her. It just seems like she's making a bad career decision, and I want to tell her how foolish she's being."

"It's natural to project our own wants and needs onto others, but Alison's wants, needs, or circumstances may be very different from yours," Blake gently pointed out. "It's why it's generally a bad idea to try to tell other people what to do."

"So, I just ignore the situation because I'm in the cheap seats?" she asked.

"Being in the cheap seats isn't wrong or bad. But knowing that's where you are when you're helping others find their way is very important. You can tell Alison you're concerned about her choice or share what you might do, but you can't assume that you know what's best for her. Instead of telling her what to do, help her explore and find her own way. Just as you're probably not emotionally involved the same way she is, she could be so overrun with emotions that she's failing to see all her options or the repercussions of her choices. Your involvement could give her clarity. If you're really interested in helping her on her journey," Blake concluded, "you should explore with her why she made her choice and help her see the pros and cons—but without judgment and from her career path instead of yours."

Kate considered this for a moment. "I can see where that makes sense. Does realizing the cheap seats work when you're taking counsel as well?"

"Of course. Frank figured that out, almost the hard way. You really want to consider the perspective of anyone 'counseling' you. Assume that they're giving you advice that's in your best interests, *in their opinion*. But remember that most people are greatly influenced by their own experiences and passions and see your world with partial scope. The challenge is that often the advice they give doesn't recognize their own limited vision. And remember, they aren't feeling what you feel—and usually can't. But what you feel matters a great deal. Always remember," Blake emphasized. "While taking in advice and feedback is good, don't let anyone who's judging from the Cheap Seats take over your game."

"This has helped quite a bit, Blake," Kate said. "I'm anxious to have another chat with Alison and let her know I'm there for her, even as she pursues this new direction."

Chapter 9

THE BELL VERSUS THE WATER

Kate walked into the coffee shop with an oversized mug in her hand. It was bright green and emblazoned with her company's logo.

"Well, that's quite . . . something, isn't it," Blake smiled.

"My assistant," Kate said, rolling her eyes. "She knows I like my coffee, so she had this made for me. She spent two hours designing it. Meanwhile, I have expense reports that should have been done weeks ago that she still hasn't completed."

"Does she do this a lot?"

Kate thought for a moment. "You know, come to think of it, she does. She's great at creative things, but not so great at more rote, detail-oriented tasks. Those, she seems to avoid like the plague. Every time we talk about this aspect of her deliverables, she always seems to take us back to these coffee cups."

"It sounds like she's focused on the Bell versus the Water."

"Wait. Before we get into another analogy, I think I need to fill this with coffee." Kate waved her oversized mug.

Taking on the Water

Carrie Shaw was at the offices of EcoClean, preparing for a series of management meetings with her fellow executives. As chief operating officer at EcoClean, she was enjoying a period of success. The large cleaning supply and service company specializing in environmentally friendly products was growing by leaps and bounds, capitalizing on the wave of interest in sustainability within the business community. Using EcoClean's products and services was an easy way to become more green.

The company's key challenge was the recruitment and retention of adequate staff at every level of the company. Carrie's job was to help them craft a multi-tiered recruitment strategy to draw employees from various pools of potential workers. This involved the marketing department, which was helping to place recruitment ads, and the IT department, which was enhancing the company's website to be more useful in attracting and soliciting applications from prospective candidates. It even involved sales, so they could offer access to their extensive network of people in the market.

However, as Carrie reviewed the report from Tom Allen, the head of human resources, she became concerned. Tom's immediate primary responsibility was to analyze the content of a survey the team had conducted with all interviewed candidates for the last three years and create recommendations for new programs and policies that would help retain talented employees and reduce turnover.

In reviewing the feedback, Tom had identified a number of needs, including the fact that the company was sorely in need of a better health care package and required mentoring, training, and other programs that would help employees grow and become more engaged.

From the report, Carrie saw that Tom was focusing his time and attention on two suggestions that had come up a couple of times in the feedback—finding new but extraneous employee benefits such as discounts to productions at the local theater and at various area restaurants and launching internal programs such as a company-sponsored team for the local Habitat for Humanity chapter's annual fundraising event.

These were helpful initiatives, and should be done, but they did little to attack the core problems identified in the exit interview feedback. It was quite clear to Carrie that the actions Tom was recommending wouldn't solve the problem and would cost precious time and resources to implement.

When Carrie arrived at Tom's office for their meeting, they exchanged a round of pleasantries about the weather and then Carrie asked Tom to walk her through the findings.

"Well, you'll see that we've been able to develop a number of new benefits. As I reviewed the exit interview data, one thing we kept hearing over and over again was that we needed better and more up-to-date benefits. So, my staff and I had a brainstorming meeting around what that meant and came up with some of the ideas you see in the report," explained Tom.

Carrie nodded. "I see that you've done quite a lot of work here, Tom. I'm sure that some of the employees will appreciate the conveniences and savings you've uncovered. But perhaps you can explain how you see this attracting more employees."

"We're really going to be getting the movie tickets at a fantastic discount. The theater started with a simple fifteen percent discount offer, and after several counter proposals, I got them to discount our tickets forty-four percent. So the price is quite good for how we'll be using the tickets."

"How will you fold this into recruiting?" Carrie asked.

Tom paused. He wasn't sure how to answer. While he understood that discount theater tickets and free meals weren't the best way to attract new employees, he had spent a great deal of time securing these benefits.

Carrie spoke again. "Tom, do you think you've focused your efforts on the true challenge here?"

Tom took a deep breath. He'd only been in his post for six months. Prior to that, he'd worked for a larger company that had many HR people. He was afraid to admit he'd never been directly involved with developing full-scale recruitment programs—his previous company usually had more resumes than it could possibly need, thanks to its high industry profile. He had little experience doing the things that needed to be done at EcoClean, and he suddenly realized, thanks to Carrie's carefully worded questions, that he was focusing on the Bell versus the Water.

Recognizing the Bell versus the Water

Deep down, Tom knew he was in over his head. He was actually quite relieved that Carrie had pursued her line of questioning, but this isn't always the case. Bringing teams or team members back in line can be a challenging process, fraught with negative feelings and denial. Team members may deflect tough questions and keep reverting to what is going well, even though it's off-topic from the direction they're receiving.

The fact is, many people gravitate to the tasks with which they're comfortable and where they've had experience or success in the past. That usually helps them ramp up quickly. The ideal situation is to find a group of people whose skills complement each other and that are applicable to the tasks at hand.

However, when one of the individuals on the team—or, sometimes, the entire team itself—pays too much attention to their strengths or to the perceived issues that need to be addressed instead of the core business needs, that can result in lots of time and attention being paid to issues that are secondary. That can be dangerous.

Conflict in these situations lies in what people do when they are either responsible for tasks with which they're not comfortable or they are afraid that the progress to date won't meet expectations. This often leads to gravitating towards tasks that are within their comfort zone but that might not add as much value or may not be the highest priority for the team or company.

While the individual focuses on those action items that are manageable and familiar because they don't understand the hierarchy of organizational needs, the rest of the team or managers may be left frustrated at what they see as a diversion. In turn, the individual may become defensive about their actions.

This sometimes becomes even more twisted when these individuals perceive that those around them are more expert at a particular task or goal. They may feel as if they have to show some sort of progress on an uncomfortable task even though they don't fully understand how to proceed.

To illustrate this phenomenon, picture the inner workings of a ship undergoing a modest retrofit while still out at sea. The captain, conducting a surprise inspection of the progress down in the engine room, sees the team hanging the new communications bell on the ceiling. He also notices about two inches of water sloshing about on the floor. The bell is a key component of the refit, and he's glad to see progress. However, he's more attracted to and concerned about the ankle deep water on the floor that's seemingly being ignored.

The captain, deeply concerned, asks the crew chief what the team is doing. She proudly explains that they've hung the bell, beaming that they're even ahead of schedule. However, when the captain points to the water on the floor and asks what is being done about that, she gives it a quick glance and says that she's sent some of her team members to look into it, but they haven't yet reported back.

The captain, partly irritated and partly confused, dismisses the review so that he might speak to the head engineer. Either the crew chief is unable to address such a dire situation or she simply doesn't see the water accumulation with the same urgency that he does. After all, their conversation makes it clear that she's focusing on the bell rather than the water.

To the captain, hanging the bell is a relatively easy task that offers some good benefits. Attacking the water requires more serious and strategic thought, but until proven otherwise, ignoring it could be quite dangerous to the ship. To the captain, it's clear that the team is opting for something they can easily understand and address, even though that decision may be putting the entire ship at peril.

Sometimes, teams do this even with the counsel of more experienced team members, people who have "sailed more ships." Instead of admitting what they don't know and either asking for help or following directions, team members or teams will take on tasks that they believe will help them shine but that aren't in tandem with the overall needs of the company.

This usually has the opposite effect. The people who are offering counsel want the team to follow direction, or at least hear it. Instead, the team tries to dazzle or impress the more senior people, resulting in conflict that diverts energy, time, and resources from the most important jobs.

To overcome the Bell versus the Water conundrum, individuals need to recognize and address the challenges at hand. Sometimes it means asking questions or requesting help when they feel like they need support, additional skills, or more information to perform the job required of them.

Other times, it means explaining current status on key issues even when progress isn't where it might be expected. Of course, this can only happen in a company culture that doesn't "shoot the messenger" for not knowing all the answers or bearing unhappy news.

The other reality might be that the crew chief understood more about why the water was there, thought it was more obvious than maybe it was, and didn't pick up on the depth of the captains concern. For her, perhaps the water was under control, and posed no real risk. So, the early progress elsewhere in the project was an appropriate focus in her conversation with the captain. In dealing with the Bell versus the Water, you need to pay attention to why a question is being asked, not just the question itself. Had she resolved the captains concern about the water, he might have been better able to celebrate the early progress on the bell.

Assisting with the Assistant

"So, when there's a Bell versus the Water situation," Blake concluded, "the most immediate need is to find ways to understand the water issue. In this case, it's your expense reports. But in the future, your assistant's approach to avoiding tasks could be something more critical to a big project or area of responsibility. She might also believe she has them under control, and has time to do extra effort on other projects."

"I'll have to think about how to approach her so that she doesn't get defensive and she can see that I'm really trying to help," said Kate. "We either have a focus issue, or at the very least a communications issue to resolve."

"Exactly. The key is to create a situation where coaching can turn the situation around. Assailing the crew that has 'hung the bell,' so to speak, will never result in a positive effect. When the team or team member is paying attention to something that doesn't matter as much, it indicates they either don't understand the more critical problems or don't know what to do about them. And if they have the water under control, you need to help them understand that it's not necessarily understood that this is the case. It's up to you and other leaders to step in and assess which of those challenges is at hand and then take steps to rectify it," said Blake.

"I guess I'm not clear on why she isn't comfortable speaking to me in the first place if she has an area that she doesn't understand. I've always thought of myself as approachable and supportive," said Kate. "But maybe its me that doesn't understand."

"Sometimes it's just a simple lack of understanding," Blake answered. "Most often, the Bell versus the Water problem is solved by instruction in the core issues facing the company. In such instances, a frank conversation to remind how the team fits into the group and company goals is necessary. This may include assigning a more senior person to monitor the situation and ensure that the individuals in question are getting back on track. But if it's an ability issue, it may be time for additional training or reorganizing the team. This can be disruptive, but not more so than allowing water to pool in the bottom of the boat."

Kate looked at her now-empty mug. "Well, one thing is for sure. She definitely understands my coffee-drinking habits."

Chapter 10

THE MONET EFFECT

When Kate walked into the coffee shop, Blake already had her order in hand.

"Light with one sugar?" he asked, handing it to her.

"Excellent. Which is more that I can say for my weekend," Kate declared as she took the cup.

"Oh, that's too bad. What happened?"

"Well, I got dragged to this exhibit at the museum. You know, the big Impressionist show that everyone is talking about? I just don't get it. It's a bunch of dots. A three-year-old could do it."

"Ah, you don't like the perspective shifts—how the works look one way from afar and another way close up?"

"Exactly. A flower should look like a flower, whether you're standing ten feet away or two feet away," Kate complained.

"Yeah, we see this in our personal lives and in business all the time, don't we?"

"What?"

"Why, it's the Monet Effect of course."

"Okay. Let me hear it," Kate said with a grin.

A Matter of Perspective

It was 7:45 a.m. at the Schilling Pharmaceuticals building, and despite the early hour, a small cluster of cars sat in the parking lot. Holly Travers and Josh Daniels, who were heading up a team to identify new marketing opportunities for blood pressure medications in the face of recent changes in pharma marketing regulations, were huddled around a conference table. Their team was becoming known for the long hours they were putting in—arriving at the office early and staying well into the evenings almost every day.

Their supervisor, Eric Marstead, appeared in the doorway.

"How's it going, gang?" he asked.

The team members looked weary, but Josh was clearly excited. "Hey, Eric. Things are great! Come join us and see what we're doing."

Eric walked in and sat down. Josh immediately began describing some of the team's current projects. As he described their efforts and approach, Eric began to see what could be a problem. He was sensing excessive required reading, and more concerning, duplicated activities going on throughout the team.

"Josh, it certainly seems like you're all busy. I'd love to sit down with you sometime soon and go over this in greater detail," he said.

They made plans to meet later that week, and Eric went to his office. On his way back, he ran into Geoff Simkins, his immediate supervisor.

"Morning, Eric. I see you were in talking with Josh and Holly's team. I'm really pleased with their dedication. They're here all the time. It's clear they're taking things seriously. I expect big things from that team. This project has to be a home run, and that means total dedication from everyone," said Geoff.

"They sure are logging the hours," said Eric. "I'm looking forward to our meeting this afternoon."

"Me, too. I think our team could learn a thing or two from that one," said Geoff, motioning toward the conference room. "We've been struggling to achieve the type of performance your team has been reaching. See you later."

Later that morning, Josh and Holly were sitting in Eric's office with laptops open and a box of files at their feet. Holly began to recount the team's activity over the past month. Eric listened to the duo's tales of meetings, reviews, team homework, and other activities. A great deal of paper fluttered about, but the actual results or conclusions were alarmingly absent.

"You seem to be putting in a lot of hours," Eric mentioned.

"No pain, no gain," Josh said with a smile.

"Have you thought about how that might be affecting your team's performance in their jobs?" Eric asked.

Josh stopped for a moment and he and Holly looked at each other. "What do you mean?" he finally asked.

"I just mean that all these extra hours might be having a negative impact on how your team members do their jobs on a daily basis. I wonder if there are ways to limit the number of hours you're spending while getting similar results," he said.

Josh seemed taken aback. "No one on the team minds," he said.

Holly shifted in her seat. Eric turned to her.

"Holly, do you agree?" he asked.

"Well. Not really."

Josh looked shocked. "What do you mean?" he asked.

Holly explained that several team members had complained to her that the hours were really starting to wear them down. It was getting harder and harder to come in each morning. They were afraid to let Josh know because he was so enthusiastic.

"But how else do we get results? We have to be committed to this; it takes this level of commitment," Josh insisted.

Eric explained to Josh that excellence isn't necessarily relative to the amount of time something takes but the results it produces. While it looked like his team was working very hard, the results weren't equivalent to the amount of time being invested.

At first, this was hard for Josh to hear, but then the conversation turned to solutions, which included delegating more individual responsibilities and eliminating duplication of work within the team. Each team member would have a specific area of responsibility instead of collaborating on every task, which would allow more progress to be made in less time. In addition, Eric told them to ask the team to put in fewer hours to prevent burnout.

At the end of the meeting, Josh and Holly were excited about the new possibilities. Later that day, Eric was in the conference room preparing for his team meeting when Geoff joined him.

"Ready for today?" Geoff asked.

"You bet," replied Eric.

"We're going to get this team in shape. I want another group like the one Holly and Josh are leading. Total dedication. Willing to put in the long hours to get big results," said Geoff.

"I think we need to talk about that," said Eric.

He explained some of the challenges he'd uncovered with Holly and Josh earlier in the day. The long hours were actually causing burnout and ineffectiveness. The team's creativity and commitment were lagging because they were tired and frustrated. They needed to log fewer hours and work smarter rather than be encouraged to stay in the office until all hours. Eric said he intended to direct this team to start off with less focus on time and more focus on results right off the bat. Geoff agreed that made sense.

The Monet Effect in Action

Geoff's perception of the team Holly and Josh led is a perfect example of the Monet Effect—the dynamic whereby a situation looks better (or worse) than it really is when viewed from a distance. Upon closer examination, we quite often discover the detail doesn't match the initial perception and there are factors we didn't see initially that make our perceptions wrong. Sometimes quite wrong.

The name "Monet" references the famous Impressionist painter whose rough brush strokes make masterpieces from a distance but look crude and ill-defined when viewed up close. It's similar to the dessert that looks great on the plate but tastes bad, or a piece of furniture that looks rather simple until you start seeing the details and discover the talent it took to build it.

In a team setting, the Monet Effect is present when a team looks like it's doing one thing or has certain capabilities and expertise but the reality is actually quite different, made visible and understandable by getting up close and really getting to know the team and their challenges.

In the case of Josh and Holly's team, it looked like their talented team of busy people were the bar setters in how to get big things done, which is exactly what Geoff was seeking. In reality, that wasn't the case, as Eric saw when he looked closely at what was really going on.

Now here's the rub with the Monet Effect. When you look at something from a distance, such as a team, person, or product, it will appear to be better or worse than it really is. With sparse information it's hard, even impossible, to really understand that thing in the distance. What determines if it's appears "better" or "worse" than it really is, is why you looked to begin with. If you're looking for a gem, you'll tend to see gems. If you're looking to prove your team is better, you'll see faults in that team out there.

Geoff was looking for a better way to get things done, and he thought he'd found it with Josh and Holly's approach. It wasn't until there was more understanding that he came to learn of some of their challenges. This doesn't mean Josh and Holly aren't onto something, but where they are now isn't where they need to be from a sustainability standpoint, and certainly isn't where Geoff perceived them to be.

We often see variations of this with teams. Looking to others for ideas, we may make snap assumptions about how much we can—or won't—learn from another team. Often, we assume that another's challenge is different or easier and that there's nothing to learn. Or we feel insecure and think another team looks "perfect", and we don't want to look inferior next to them.

It's only when we understand their true strengths and weaknesses that we can really learn from them. Only then can we ask ourselves what we can take away that's good, and what lessons these teams have to teach us about pitfalls.

Similarly, if a team boasts about its achievements, there may be an assumption that other teams don't have the same level of challenge, that their accomplishments don't "count" or aren't as significant as the more pedigreed or challenged team. However, beneath the surface, there are always challenges or strengths that aren't immediately visible.

That, again, is the Monet Effect. From a distance, we think we understand the components of the picture, but it looks very different when examined up close. In addition, our initial motivation for making the comparison has an impact on what we see in the distance because it's influenced by our perceptions or preferences.

Another area where this dynamic is frequently seen is in interactions between team leaders or supervisors and team members. If team members don't feel comfortable speaking up about their concerns or confusion, it may seem as if the team is working together well, but that isn't really the case. Teams that do not have clear and open communication protocols and expectations may find that members are not fully "on board" with the team's mission, and as a result, are either unwilling or unable to fully carry out their duties. From the manager's perspective, the goal is a well-run team filled with happy, contributing members, and it can be easy to assume that silence indicates they're running well.

That's why, when managing a team, it's important to watch for signs that team members are holding back. This may not be evident until you truly study the team closely—remember those individual brush strokes that make up the masterpiece?

When team members aren't giving their all, it's important to take a closer look and try to understand why. If that doesn't happen, disconnects occur that can jeopardize the team's ability to succeed. We might see the effect in how managers absentmindedly favor certain team members or think of other team members almost as "troubled children." The manager may rely more or put more pressure on the "chosen ones" because they consistently produce better, but in reality, those perceptions may be inaccurate. These team members have highs and lows just like everyone else. Such perceptions may also fail to capitalize on the talents of those who are not "chosen ones."

The Art of Seeing Things Clearly

"So, you have to be careful and understand that your own perspective and motivation will skew your ability to understand the reality and quality of the work or the people," Kate concluded.

"That's exactly right. There was one time when I was running a technical team," Blake reflected. "A team from another department was also doing some good work and offered to share some of their processes with us. But my team thought they knew everything they needed to know about the deployment of a new product line. When I suggested we look at some interdepartmental teams to see if there were improvements that could be made, the team didn't agree, so I let it drop."

"What happened?"

"Several months later, that team beat us for a company-wide award. We could have definitely learned a few things from them."

"So how can you correct the Monet Effect?"

"Spot-check your teams from time to time. Take a more careful and measured look at team members' actions, engagement, and results. Judging the team from a distance is where you can get into trouble, as is making assumptions. After all, if you don't live in Texas and you have no idea what life in Texas is like, you may still have some assumptions about what it must be like to reside there. And while some of the assumptions may be correct, others are going to be wildly inaccurate. However, you won't know which is which until you experience it for yourself, or get someone to share specific details of their experiences, not just the good or the bad," Blake explained.

"Right," Kate agreed. "That's what happened with Geoff when it came to his evaluations of Josh, Holly, and their team. He was looking for a 'super-performing team' and assumed the hours logged from a distance were a good indicator. He wasn't paying attention to the fine detail of the team's burnout and their ineffective results."

"Exactly. And as you said, given that he was looking for a better performing team, he found one with Eric's team. Even though this wasn't really the case, as he later learned when he stepped closer."

Kate considered for a moment. "This makes perfect sense when I think about times I've managed my team's interactions with others. Heck, it makes perfect sense when I think about myself. It's easy to get psyched out thinking the new guy is so much better than me, even before I really know him."

"Exactly," confirmed Blake. "You always want to bring the situation into proper perspective before finalizing judgment. This is especially the case when you're certain, yet you have sparse information. That's when the Monet Effect will be in play the most."

Chapter 11

CONCLUSION

Analogies can be very effective in getting a message across. Next time a Ball of Energy comes your way, or for that matter a Pizza Statement, take a deep breath. Stop and think. Before you act or react to those around you, think about how you're Managing Your Tokens. Do you need to manage them better? Don't feel bad if you're tempted to Eat the Cricket. It might just be the right food for you. But beware of Digging the Perfect Hole in the Wrong Place, or not delivering that Ten-Pound Job. Try your best not to be guilty of judging from the Cheap Seats, and remember that others are advising you from them all the time. Remember the pitfalls inherent in the Water versus the Bell, and do your very best not to have clear judgment, even in the face of the Monet Effect.

No doubt these analogies are recognizable from your own experience. Perhaps you see a former boss or work situation. You may recognize team members or even people in your personal life. Maybe you even see yourself.

These analogies resonate because they illustrate common themes and circumstances that we likely encounter at one point or another as we interact with those around us. By being more aware of the challenges and pitfalls that await us, and understanding the real drivers behind them, we can begin to reduce the damage from missteps in the choices we make and even eliminate those missteps in the first place. We can act and react with far better precision for ourselves and those around us by keeping our eyes open.

You may also recognize Blake in these analogies. He's the embodiment of the collective wisdom and experience that helps us recognize team challenges both in ourselves and others. When we see how our choices can have a negative impact on our careers and the projects in which we're involved, we are more likely to temper them and be mindful of the things we say and do and the ways we interact with those around us.

When we recognize bad or thoughtless behavior in others, especially through the objective and somewhat removed lens of these analogies, we can begin to evaluate the best course of action to deal with such behaviors while preserving our team relationships and maintaining the power of the team where it belongs—driving projects forward.

Analogies are very powerful tools when used in the right way, at the right time, to help us more clearly see issues when they arise. The analogies here have intentionally simple, sometimes playful, names. By sharing them with those around you and utilizing them in your interactions, you can greatly reduce the anxiety of giving someone potentially challenging feedback. And once incorporated into your team's language, you can both challenge and express ideas a lot quicker. You can now ask powerful questions like, "Did I manage that Ball of Energy in a way that will help my employee know I care about his long-term success?" or "All the Pizza Statements flying around are kind of throwing us off track" or "I think we need to get to know them better. Right now I think the Monet Effect is at work here."

How will you use these analogies? It is my hope that you will teach them to your team members and integrate them into your daily conversations. In so doing, you will give each other a non-inflammatory shorthand to help mitigate the damage that these common speed bumps can cause. For example, when someone throws around a careless statement claiming to be the best, calling out "Pizza!" can be a humorous but effective way of stopping it in its tracks.

Similarly, reminding an employee or fellow team member to "Dig the hole in the right place" can be a helpful and gentle way of redirecting efforts that should be focused elsewhere.

Think about your own current team situations. Which analogies apply? Which could you put in place tomorrow? How would doing so impact your team and your ability to help it achieve its goals?

As you apply these analogies to your work and personal lives, I invite you to share your success stories and challenges with me. I have taught these lessons to people around the world, and they have made many individuals and teams more effective. As you find they begin to work for you, or if you have questions, stories, or your own analogies to share, please contact me directly at Peter@ChooseNotToFail.Com.

Finally, thank you for your interest in this book. Keep your eyes open and see opportunities for greater efficiency and harmony in virtually everything you do.

ABOUT THE AUTHOR

After a nearly twenty-year career at Microsoft contributing to some of the world's most famous software solutions, in the fall of 2010 Peter Jerkewitz moved to the next stage in his career by starting NovusWorks. In this new venture, he's continuing with his passion of working with individuals, organizations, and leaders to enable better business delivery while helping individuals find their best career path and performance.

He's served as leader and manager for much of his career and values the role greatly. For Peter, working with people to help them find themselves and align their passions to real business needs—to the benefit of themselves personally while producing fantastic business results for customers—is really what it's all about. He brings this passion and insight into nearly every conversation in which he's involved.

Today Peter lives on the U.S. east coast. He enjoys traveling and experiencing different areas, people, and cultures of the world. He also spends time exploring and understanding history from around the world.

If you'd like to chat with Peter, feel free to email him at Peter@ChooseNotToFail.Com. He'd enjoy learning about your applications and impressions of the stories in this book.